# AMAZING BUT TRUE SPORTS STORIES

Phyllis and Zander Hollander

Illustrated with photographs

An Associated Features Book

SCHOLASTIC INC.
New York Toronto London Auckland Sydney

ACKNOWLEDGMENTS: The collection of stories in this book came from many sources—alert friends who spotted something unusual, fellow sportswriters, the wire services, newspapers, and magazines. The authors acknowledge with appreciation all those who inspired the many bits and pieces and authenticated *Amazing But True Sports Stories*.

PHOTO CREDITS: 6, 10,13, 43,63,85,90,130: Wide World. 16, 20, 38: Sports Photo Service. 30, 51, 52, 54, 58, 123: UPI. 31: Cincinnati Reds. 44: St. Louis Cardinals. 46: Mitchell B. Reibel. 47: MGM. 67: North Central College. 71: Vic Milton. 74: Kevin W. Reece. 80: The Chuck Connors Collection. 99: *The Seattle Times*. 100: Steve Babineau. 108: Richard Pilling.

ISBN 0-590-33377-1

12 11 10 9 8 7 6 5 4                    8 9/8 0 1/9

# CONTENTS

# Introduction

The real fascination in sports is in the unpredictable. No matter what game it is, something unusual, bizarre, startling, strange, unexpected . . . amazing can occur.

It could be the star outfielder who gets hit by a runaway tarpaulin, or a schoolboy who pitches lefty . . . and righty.

It could be a Super Bowl MVP who falls asleep at a fancy dinner in Washington after insulting an Associate Justice of the Supreme Court of the United States; a running back who becomes a star in television's *Hill Street Blues;* the coach who springs from the sidelines in a game and tackles an enemy ball-carrier; or the college that has four and a half sets of twins in its lineup.

It could be a one-armed basketball player; a 52-year-old right wing in the National Hockey League; a marathon runner who takes a short

1

cut to the finish line; or a wrestler who comes back from Hodgkins disease to win an Olympic gold medal.

They are all in *Amazing But True Sports Stories*, a collection of 87 stories covering odd happenings in a variety of sports.

Some are humorous, some are sad. There are heroes and villains. There are miracles and there are hoaxes.

But no matter how amazing, all of these stories really happened.

*Phyllis and Zander Hollander*

# BASEBALL

### Going, Going, Gone

They say that what goes up must come down. Well, not always.

There was this major-league game on May 4, 1984, at the Hubert H. Humphrey Metrodome in Minneapolis. Oakland was playing the Minnesota Twins.

With two out in the fourth inning, Minnesota pitcher Frank Viola threw a low fastball to Dave Kingman. The batter they call "King Kong"—because of his size and mighty wallops—hit what appeared to be a routine high pop-up over the infield.

Minnesota shortstop Houston Jiminez and third baseman John Castino stood behind the mound, gazing upward. Jiminez called for the ball. He waited. Then he waited some more.

"When nothing was coming down, I got

scared," Jiminez said. "I covered my head. Never in my life had I seen anything like this. It was amazing."

Castino said, "It was the most helpless feeling. We just waited and waited . . . three, four, five seconds."

The ball, it turned out, had disappeared through a drainage hole in the bottom layer of the Metrodome's fabric ceiling, about 180 feet above home plate.

Umpire Jim Evans gave Kingman a ground-rule double, citing as precedent the double he had once granted when a ball lodged in a rooftop speaker in Seattle's Kingdome.

## Two-Way Pitcher

Steve Butz, a pitcher at Central Catholic High School in Lafayette, Indiana, has his eyes and both arms set on a trail that could lead to the major leagues.

Butz throws right-handed and left-handed, meaning he's a switch-pitcher, a breed so rare that *The Baseball Encyclopedia* lists only one such hurler in major-league history.

He was Tony Mullane, whose nicknames were "Count" and "The Apollo of the Box." Mullane, born in Cork, Ireland, in 1859, pitched lefty and righty for 13 years in the late 1800's.

His won-lost record was 285-215, with an earned-run average of 3.05.

Butz is a natural left-hander, but his three older brothers were right-handers and he wound up using their gloves. So, by necessity, he got into the habit of learning to throw right-handed.

"I guess I pitch a little harder with my left, but my right has better control," Butz told William Barnhardt of *Sports Illustrated*.

Butz usually starts as a lefty and after a few innings he switches. As a 15-year-old in 1985, he hadn't yet switched arms in the same inning, or on the same batter. But there's no law that says he can't do that.

### Phil Niekro's Astounding Switch

It came down to the final game of the 1985 baseball season. In his previous four appearances on the mound, the New York Yankees' Phil Niekro had failed to win his 300th game in a career that had begun with Milwaukee in 1964.

The Yankees were playing the Toronto Blue Jays, the team that had beaten them out of the American League East pennant. Only 17 players in major-league history had ever won 300 games when the 46-year-old right-hander

*The Yankees' Phil Niekro had a surprise in store for the Toronto Blue Jays when he went after his 300th victory.*

took the mound in Toronto. From the time he began in the majors, Niekro had primarily thrown the knuckleball, and the Blue Jays were prepared to blitz Niekro's best pitch.

Though out of the pennant race, the Yankees were determined to give Niekro all the support he needed. They got off to a three-run lead in the first inning and Niekro responded by giving up only one hit in the first six innings and only three more in the course of the game. The Yankees wound up as 8-0 victors.

But what was most remarkable was the fact that the great knuckleballer did not throw a knuckleball until there were two out in the ninth inning.

"I always wanted to pitch a whole game without throwing a knuckleball, because people thought I couldn't get anyone out without doing so," Niekro said after the game.

He finally threw three knuckleballs to Jeff Burroughs, striking him out with the third one for the final out of his 300th victory.

"I figured there was no other way to finish the game than to use the pitch that got me there," Niekro said.

# A Tale of Two Cities

It was a day full of surprises for Joel Youngblood. After he hit a third-inning two-run single that would help the New York Mets defeat the Chicago Cubs on August 5, 1982, he was told he'd been traded to the Montreal Expos.

This was in the afternoon at Chicago's Wrigley Field. Youngblood promptly went back to the hotel and made plane reservations for Philadelphia, where the Expos were playing that night. Then he realized he'd left his glove in the dugout at Wrigley Field. He raced back to the ball park, barely making his plane.

When he arrived in Philadelphia, the Phillies-Expos game was in the third inning. Youngblood donned his new uniform and Montreal manager Jim Fanning wasted no time inserting Youngblood into right field. Youngblood proceeded to get a single in the Expos' 5-4 loss to the Phillies.

Youngblood thus tied the major-league record for most teams played within one day (two), set by Max Flack and Cliff Heathcote, who were traded by the St. Louis Cardinals and Chicago Cubs between games of a doubleheader on May 30, 1922.

# A Royal Flush

Only three years earlier he was pitching in high school. Now 21-year-old Bret Saberhagen was in the World Series, on the mound for the Kansas City Royals against the St. Louis Cardinals.

The Royals had been behind, three games to one, but they'd come back to tie the Series, forcing a seventh and final game at Kansas City on October 27, 1985.

For Saberhagen, a 6-foot, 160-pound right-hander, there had been cause for celebration the day before: His wife gave birth to their first child.

He had all the incentive he needed as, inning by inning, he silenced the Cardinal bats. Meanwhile, the Royals, led by Darryl Motley, George Brett, and Steve Balboni, were off to a blazing start with five runs in the first three innings.

Things got so frustrating for St. Louis that starting pitcher John Tudor smashed an electric fan in the Cardinal clubhouse after he was knocked out of the box in the third inning. He suffered a cut on his left index finger. The Cards' fiery-tempered Joaquin Andujar, pitching in relief, had to be dragged away from an umpire after objecting to a call during the

*Bret Saberhagen and George Brett celebrate the Kansas City Royals' winning of the 1985 World Series against the St. Louis Cardinals.*

Royals' six-run fifth inning. And Cards' manager Whitey Herzog, as well as Andujar, was ejected.

All in all, it was a bizarre game that saw Saberhagen pitch a five-hitter as the Royals flushed the Cardinals, 11-0, for the World Championship.

The Royals became only the fifth team in World Series history to win a best-of-seven series after losing three of the first four games, and they were the first to do so after losing the first two games at home.

It was a remarkable comeback and Saberhagen, who'd been a winner in Game 3, was named World Series Most Valuable Player, the youngest ever.

## What a Way To Go

Mark Lee was a sinkerball pitcher who can always say that he had four years in the major leagues — with San Diego and Pittsburgh. It's all in *The Baseball Encyclopedia* — 118 games, 7-8 won-lost, and 3.63 earned-run average.

But this independent reliefman will be known more for what he did in the Pacific Coast League on August 16, 1982. Entering a game for the Portland Beavers against Vancouver in the top of the ninth inning, he got the first out on a pop-up and the second on a strikeout. Then he called manager Tom Trebelhorn to the mound.

"Nothing against you, Treb," he said, "but I'd rather go out this way.

Whereupon he trudged off the mound, stopped to throw the ball back to the infield, and headed for the exit, tossing his cap into the air and removing his jersey.

Before the game he had been told he would be released by the Beavers, a Pittsburgh farm team. "This was my last hurrah," he explained. "It was my way of saying, 'You guys can control some of the things, but you can't control all of the things in my life.'"

## A Cobb-Rose Coincidence

The pitcher was Eric Show of the San Diego Padres.

The batter was Pete Rose of the Cincinnati Reds.

The clocks at Cincinnati's Riverfront Stadium flashed exactly 8:00 as Rose went through his ritual — a tap of the right spike with his bat, a push on his red battling helmet to shove it firmly over his head.

The first pitch was a ball, high and outside. Rose took a massive swing at the next pitch, fouling it over the backstop. Then Show threw high and inside for ball two.

Now Rose waved his bat toward Show and dipped into his familiar low crouch, peering intently at the pitcher.

*Pete Rose's record-breaking hit celebrated a Ty Cobb anniversary.*

It was 8:01. Show threw again. Rose swung firmly and the ball sped safely into right field. And 47,237 spectators went wild.

Peter Edward Rose, 44, streaks of gray through his hair, stood alone. He had posted hit No. 4,192, breaking Ty Cobb's all-time hit record.

It happened on September 11, 1985 — exactly 57 years to the day when Ty Cobb made his last plate appearance.

# Marathon Game

It would prove to be a game like no other in history.

It began on April 18, 1981, a cold, windy night at McCoy Stadium in Pawtucket, Rhode Island. The Pawtucket Red Sox were playing the Rochester Red Wings in the International League.

Rochester scored the first run in the seventh inning and Pawtucket tied it up in the ninth. The game went into extra innings, but there was no score until Rochester got a run in the 21st inning. However, Pawtucket did the same to keep the game knotted at 2-2.

And it went on and on and on.

"By the thirtieth inning," Pawtucket owner Ben Mondor said, "I was really starting to be concerned about the players being so groggy. Somebody might get hurt."

By then the Pawtucket manager, Joe Morgan, was sitting under the stands with some of the players' wives and children, many of whom were asleep. Morgan had been ejected in the 21st inning for disputing an umpire's call.

Around 3 A.M., Mike Tamburro, the Pawtucket publicity man, phoned International League commissioner Harold Cooper, who lives in Columbus, Ohio. "We're still playing," Tamburro said.

"You can't still be playing," Cooper insisted.

The game was about to enter the bottom of the 32nd inning. Cooper, fully awake by now, told Jack Lietz, chief of the umpire crew, "If it's still tied at the end of the inning, suspend the game."

Deadlocked at 2-2 after 32 innings and a total playing time of eight hours and seven minutes, the game was suspended at 4:07 A.M., to be resumed on June 22.

When play was resumed two months later, the entire baseball world seemed to be focused on Pawtucket. More than 50 newspapers, three television networks, and numerous radio stations from as far away as Japan were on hand to witness this bizarre event.

But the suspense came to a swift end when Pawtucket's Dave Koza singled home the winning run in the 33rd inning. The marathon was finally settled after 8 hours and 25 minutes of playing time, 67 days after it had begun.

Cal Ripken Jr., the Rochester third baseman, on the way to stardom with the Baltimore Orioles, had two hits in 13 at-bats. Pawtucket's Wade Boggs, who would later become an American League batting champion with the Boston Red Sox, went 4-for-12.

In the process the International League teams surpassed the previous organized-baseball record of 29 innings played by Miami and St. Petersburg in the Florida State League on June 14, 1966. (Miami won, 4-3.) And they outdistanced the major-league record of 26 innings, the 1-1 tie played by the Brooklyn Dodgers and Boston Braves on May 2, 1920.

## The Great One

He represented one of the big mistakes in Dodger history. They were then the Brooklyn Dodgers and they signed Roberto Clemente out of his native Puerto Rico in 1953. But the Dodgers made him available in the draft and the Pittsburgh Pirates quickly picked him up.

Clemente became one of the greatest right fielders in the game, winning the National League batting championship four times, Most Valuable Player in 1966, and was chosen to the All-Star team 12 times in 18 years. His career batting average was .317 and he hit 240 homers.

Not only did he have an outstanding throwing arm, he was a smart runner, and for 12 consecutive years he was named to the league Gold Glove All-Star fielding team.

In the 1971 World Series Clemente batted .414 and was voted MVP as the Pirates beat the Baltimore Orioles. The following year, in the final regular-season game, Clemente became the 11th player in history to achieve 3,000 career hits.

On New Year's Eve, 1972, the man who was known in Puerto Rico as "The Great One" boarded a small plane carrying supplies to victims of an earthquake in Nicaragua. The

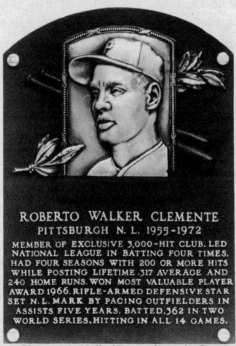

*Roberto Clemente's Hall of Fame plaque in Cooperstown, New York.*

plane crashed and Clemente, humanitarian and ballplayer, died tragically at the age of 38.

## Runaway Tarpaulin

Vince Coleman, the base-stealing champion of the 1985 St. Louis Cardinals, was doing stretching exercises on the artificial turf of St. Louis' Busch Memorial Stadium. This was on October 13, 1985, before the fourth game of the National League play-off series against the Los Angeles Dodgers.

It started to rain, the batting cage was wheeled away by the ground crew, and Coleman continued to stretch. Meanwhile, a ground-crew member pulled the lever to activate the 120-foot hydraulic cylinder that rolls the canvas tarpaulin covering for the infield. When activated, the tarpaulin automatically unrolls.

Coleman didn't see it. The cylinder rolled behind him and knocked him down, bruising his foot and knee. He was carried off the field and treated by the team physician. But the fleet-footed rookie outfielder who had stolen 110 bases during the season was unable to play.

As it developed, he'd suffered a bone chip in his left knee. He was finished for the season. The bizarre accident resulted in Tito Landrum replacing Coleman, and he emerged as the unexpected star who helped the Cardinals to victory in the play-offs and went on to bat .360 in the World Series won by the Kansas City Royals.

## The Odd Couple

The New York Mets were leading, 1-0, top of the ninth, with three Pittsburgh Pirates on base, nobody out. There were 33,610 fans at Shea Stadium. It was June 27, 1967.

The Pirates' Bill Mazeroski stepped to the plate. The count went to 2 and 2 and then he grounded into a triple play. Precisely what Neil (Doc) Simon had ordered.

The triple play happened before the start of a regularly scheduled Mets-Pirates game and was staged for a scene in *The Odd Couple*, the film adaptation of playwright Simon's Broadway comedy.

In the film, the segment marked a dramatic climax to the odd-couple relationship of sportswriter Oscar Madison (Walter Matthau) and his roommate Felix Unger (Jack Lemmon). At the time of the triple play, Matthau received a phone call from Lemmon, who told Matthau not to eat any frankfurters since that's what they were having for dinner.

In the press box Matthau was so involved with the phone call that he missed seeing the triple play. "It was the first time I ever saw a triple play and I didn't see it," Matthau moaned.

*Walter Matthau gets the dinner menu from Jack Lemmon in* The Odd Couple.

# The Natural

Readers of *Sports Illustrated* opened their April 1, 1985 issue to read an amazing story about one Haden (Sidd) Finch, reportedly a pitching prospect in spring training with the New York Mets.

The writer of the story, George Plimpton, quoted the Mets' scouting report as saying, "He's unbelievable! Could be the phenom of all time."

"The Met front office is reluctant to talk about Finch," Plimpton wrote. "The fact is, they know very little about him. He has had no baseball career. Most of his life has been spent abroad, except for a short period at Harvard University."

Plimpton's report revealed that Finch had spent his early childhood in an orphanage in Leicester, England, and he was adopted by a foster parent, archaeologist Francis Whyte-Finch, who was killed in an airplane crash in the Himalayas.

Finch withdrew from Harvard in the spring of 1976, according to Plimpton, and nothing was heard of him until he showed up in the summer of 1984 at Old Orchard Beach, Maine, where the Mets' AAA farm club, the Tidewater

Tides, was in town for a series against the Guides.

"I was strolling back to the hotel," said Bob Schaefer, the Tides' manager, "when suddenly this guy — nice-looking kid, clean-shaven, blue jeans, big boots — appears alongside. At first I think maybe he wants an autograph, or to chat about the game. But no, he scrabbles around in a kind of knapsack, gets out a scuffed-up baseball and a small, black leather fielder's mitt that looks like it came out of the back of some Little League kid's closet. This guy says to me, 'I have learned the art of the pitch. . . .'

"I am about to hurry on to the hotel when this kid points out a soda bottle on top of a fence about the same distance home plate is from the pitcher's rubber. He rears way back, comes around, and pops the ball at it. Out there on that fence post the soda bottle explodes. It disintegrates like a rifle bullet hit it. . . . I said, very calm, 'Son, would you mind showing me that again?' And he did. It wasn't the accuracy of the pitch so much that got to me, but the *speed*. I thought to myself, My God, that kid's thrown the ball about one hundred fifty miles per hour. Nolan Ryan's fastball is a change-up compared to what this kid throws."

Finch tells the manager he knows the rules and that he learned to pitch by flinging rocks and meditating in Tibet. Finch says he's not sure he wants to play big-league baseball, but he'd like to give it a try.

The Mets invite Finch to spring training in 1985, but Finch writes back with a number of stipulations, according to Plimpton. Among them are that he "would show the Mets his pitching prowess in privacy and that the whole operation in St. Petersburg was to be kept as secret as possible, with no press or photographs."

The Mets agree to Finch's stipulations and Mel Stottlemyre, the Met pitching coach, is put in charge of Finch's tryout. To keep secrecy, Finch pitches in a canvas enclosure, with such tight security that even Met players are shooed away. But Met manager Davey Johnson has seen him throw about half a dozen pitches.

"If he didn't have that great control, he'd be like the Terminator out there," Johnson says. "Hell, that fastball, if off-target on the inside, would carry a batter's kneecap into the catcher's mitt."

Plimpton relates that *Sports Illustrated* contacted Baseball Commissioner Peter Ueberroth and told him about this kid who could throw the ball over 150 miles per hour. "Roll that by me again," Ueberroth says. "I'll have to see it to believe it."

Response to the *Sports Illustrated* article was unbelievable. The baseball world couldn't wait to see this phenom. But they'll never see him. Author Plimpton's article appeared in the April Fool's issue. The whole thing was a hoax.

## Double Heave-Ho

In his distinguished career as manager of the Baltimore Orioles, fiery Earl Weaver has drawn his share of suspensions and been thrown out of many a game for arguing with the umpires.

But on September 30, 1985, Weaver outdid himself during a doubleheader against New York at Yankee Stadium. He started early in the first game, contesting a first-inning bunt that was ruled foul and contending that Yankee catcher Butch Wynegar failed to tag Floyd Rayford after dropping a called strike. Both incidents resulted in lengthy arguments, but the umpires didn't eject Weaver.

In the third inning, Yankee pitcher Jim

Cowley was struck on the hand by a shot hit by Jim Dwyer. Yankee coach Bill Monobouquette came out to check Cowley's hand and Weaver bounded from the dugout to ask if the Yankees had been charged with a visit to the mound. Weaver apparently said some other things that caused chief umpire Jim Evans to throw Weaver out of the game.

Just before the second game, Weaver again confronted Evans, claiming that Evans had said he'd meet Weaver in the parking lot after the game and "kick his butt." Evans not only denied the charge, but he ejected Weaver from the second game.

It was Weaver's 93rd career ejection and marked his first double heave-ho.

## The Great Pine Tar Incident

**Yankee Stadium,** July 24, 1983. Two out in the top of the ninth. The Yankees lead the Royals, 4-3. U.L. Washington singles. George Brett socks a Goose Gossage fastball into the lower deck in right field. The Royals win, 5-4.

Hold it! Yankee manager Billy Martin runs out to home-plate umpire Tim McClelland and demands that Brett's bat be checked for excessive pine tar. That's the substance batters apply to their bats to give them a better grip. Baseball rules say that the bat handle may not be covered for more than 18 inches from the end.

Umpire McClelland measures and determines that it's more than 18 inches. Suddenly he thrusts his right arm in the air, signaling that Brett is out. The home run doesn't count. The Yankees win, 4-3.

Hold it! Less than a week later American League president Lee MacPhail, noting that the rules do not provide that a hitter be called out for excessive use of the tar, reverses the umpire's decision. He calls for the game to be resumed later in the season if it affects the pennant race — with the Royals leading, 5-4, two out, in their half of the ninth.

Twenty-one days later, the Yankees and the Royals finish the game. The Royals' Hal McRae strikes out and the Yankees get to bat in the bottom of the ninth. Three men come up, three go down. Kansas City wins, 5-4, and at last "The Great Pine Tar Incident" is over.

# The Pitcher Who Became a Priest

Baseball fans have discovered that their heroes, like many Americans, carry union cards and occasionally go on strike.

In 1912, however, there was no union when the game's best hitter, Detroit's Ty Cobb, was suspended by American League president Ban Johnson for climbing into the stands in New York and pummeling a heckler. But Cobb's Tiger teammates stood behind him and vowed not to play until he was reinstated.

Since a $5,000 fine was the penalty for a forfeit, Hughie Jennings, the Detroit manager, rounded up a collection of college students and sandlot players from St. Joseph's College in Philadelphia. They were signed to one-game contracts.

One of the St. Joseph's players was Aloysius (Allan) Travers, whose misfortune it was to be the pitcher. He had to go against a Detroit team that had won the world championship in each of the two previous seasons.

Travers pitched the entire game. When he walked off the mound, he had been charged with 24 runs, 10 unearned. He allowed 26 hits, walked seven, and struck out one. The final score was 24-2.

The embarrassment was such for all that

the next day's game was postponed and Johnson reinstated Cobb so that the travesty would not be repeated.

And Travers, enlightened by his experience, entered the priesthood.

His name stands, however, in the record book. Never has one pitcher yielded as many runs in a single game.

## Called on Account of Grasshoppers

A horde of grasshoppers, numbering in the millions, invaded the Texas League baseball park in Midland, Texas, during the second game of a doubleheader between Midland and Amarillo.

The grasshoppers hit in such numbers that they dimmed the lights. Fans screamed, players swung their bats, and everyone clawed at the insects covering the playing field, the stands, and the mercury vapor lights.

The umpires were forced to suspend the game.

Health Department officials said a cool weather front that had pushed into the area might have brought the invasion.

# A 15-Year-Old Major-Leaguer

It was in 1944, during World War II. In every labor market, including baseball, they were saying the same line: "We've reached the bottom of the manpower barrel." Most able-bodied men were off to war.

To fill their rosters, major-league teams were signing long-retired players, some of them in their forties. At the time Joe Nuxhall was a schoolboy in Hamilton, Ohio, where he pitched in baseball and played basketball.

The left-handed Nuxhall also played in a Sunday league with older players. He was so impressive that a scout for the Cincinnati Reds signed him to a contract—$175 a month with a $500 bonus. But the Reds kept it a secret until after Nuxhall's sophomore year was over. The newspaper headline read: "Reds Sign 15-Year-Old Wonder."

Nuxhall sat on the bench for a few games, wondering if he would ever get to play. The Reds, who were going nowhere in that 1944 season, were playing the pennant-bound St. Louis Cardinals at old Crosley Field in Cincinnati on June 12, 1944. They were taking a beating. After seven and a half innings, the Cardinals led, 13-0.

As the home eighth began, young Joe sat

*Joe Nuxhall: 15 years old and a Cincinnati Red.*

*Nuxhall throws in batting practice in the 1980's.*

at one end of the dugout. Max McKechnie, the Reds' manager, was at the opposite end.

"I was just thrilled to be there," Nuxhall recalls. "My mind was on my first trip as a major-leaguer. After the game we would be taking the train to Chicago. Suddenly I heard Mr. McKechnie yell, 'Joe.' I thought he was calling one of our catchers. But he was talking to me. 'Kid, warm up, you're going in.' I couldn't believe it."

Within minutes Nuxhall was on the mound in his first major-league game—at 15 the youngest ever to play in the big leagues. He got the first batter on a ground ball, walked the next one, then got a pop-up on the third. The next batter walked and Stan Musial, a future Hall of Famer, came to the plate. Musial ducked away from one pitch and then singled in a run. By the time the inning was over, Nuxhall had given up five runs on five walks and two singles, and had faced the entire Cardinal batting order.

He never got to Chicago—at least not that season. Nuxhall was sent to the minor leagues to get experience and he didn't get back to the major leagues until eight years later. And then he became a full-fledged major-leaguer, pitching for 16 years through 1966. Nuxhall posted a career won-lost record of 135-117, with an earned-run average of 3.90.

What is further intriguing is that Nuxhall still pitches today — in batting practice for the Reds — before heading to the broadcast booth, where he has been the team's analyst on the air for two decades.

But he is best remembered for that summer day in 1944 when he made baseball history.

### A Letter to Babe Ruth

As president of the American League, an irate Ban Johnson struck out the mighty Babe Ruth.

Chicago, Ill., June 21, 1922

*Mr. George H. Ruth*
*c/o Brunswick Hotel*
*Boston, Mass.*
*Dear Sir:*
*There is a period in the trend of affairs when forbearance ceases to be a virtue. In your struggling moments to regain your prestige in the ranks of your profession, much indulgence was shown you. This plainly you did not understand, and you again have overreached the point of consideration and the hope of thoughts of those who tried to bring you into the line of usefulness and worthy endeavor.*

*I was keenly disappointed and amazed when I received Umpire Dinneen's report, recounting your shameful and abusive language to that official in the game at Cleveland last Monday.*

*Bill Dinneen was one of the greatest pitchers the game ever produced, and with common consent we hand to him today the just tribute. He is one of the cleanest and most honorable men baseball ever fostered.*

*The American League is a stern and unrelenting organization. It has a clear conception of its duty toward the public. Any departure from sportsmanship, fair play, and decency will be sharply rebuked. Your conduct at Cleveland on Monday was reprehensible to a great degree — shocking to every American mother who permits her boy to go to a professional game.*

*The American League cares nothing for Ruth. The individual player means nothing to the organization. When he steps on the ballfield he is subject to our control and discipline. It is a leading question as to whether it is permissable to allow a man of your influence and breeding to continue in the game. The evidence is at hand that you have willfully betrayed two of the most enterprising and indulgent club owners in the game.*

*Again you offended on Tuesday. You branded Umpire Dinneen as "yellow." This is the most remarkable declaration a modern ball player has made. Dinneen stands out in the history of the game as one of the most courageous players we have ever had. If you could match up to his standard you would not be in the trough you occupy today. A man of your stamp bodes no good in the profession.*

*I have a thorough knowledge of your misconduct where you dragged your teammates to a violation of club rules absolutely at variance with discipline and loyalty. What I have in my possession I will later submit to President Ruppert and Col. Huston.*

*It would be the height of folly to condone the things you have done. In the history of baseball there was never another player who drew the enormous salary your contract calls for this year. You are plainly not earning your money, and your prestige has sunk to a standard where you are of no particular value to the New York club.*

*Coupled with your misconduct on Monday, you doubled the penalty on Tuesday. You are hereby notified of your suspension for five (5) days without salary. It seems the period has arrived when you should allow some intelligence to creep into a mind that has plainly been warped.*

*I am*

*Yours truly,*
*B.B. Johnson*

## And the Band Played On

Pitcher Sparky Lyle hadn't signed his Yankee contract as it neared time for spring training in 1978. Sparky was unhappy with his limited playing time and with owner George Steinbrenner.

Several days late, he and his wife decided to head for spring training anyway. When they got off the plane at Fort Lauderdale, Florida, they saw the 100-piece marching band from Hollywood Hills High school — complete with cheerleaders and pompon girls. And the band played "Pomp and Circumstance."

They wondered what the occasion was. Then they saw a sign reading WELCOME HOME, SPARKY LYLE — FINALLY.

And Sparky realized what was happening.

"I couldn't have done better myself," he said, acknowledging this would have to go high on his all-time list of practical jokes. A practical joker himself, Sparky vowed, "I'll get the one responsible for this."

As he soon discovered, the idea was Steinbrenner's, an attempt at a peace offering. They made their peace — for a season — and the next year Sparky was a Texas Ranger.

# Little Men

And now, finally, a replacement for Eddie Gaedel, the 3-foot-7 pinch hitter who batted once for the St. Louis Browns in 1951 and walked on four pitches.

His successor — on a scholastic level — is Brian Bujduso, a 4-foot-11 freshman at Andrean High in Merrillville, Indiana. Bujduso tried out for the junior-varsity team in the spring of 1985, but had to settle for being the team's student manager.

His coach, Dave Pishkur, gave him a uniform and a chance to work out with the team. And one day Bujduso was given a chance to bat with the bases loaded. Bujduso was told not to swing at anything. And Bujduso walked on five pitches.

On the heels of such success, Bujduso was called on five other times as a pinch-hitter. Twice he got walks. The other times he was removed for a pinch-hitter after looking at two strikes. Not once in 27 pitches did he swing at the ball.

Bujduso will never be as famous as Eddie Gaedel, but at least he won his varsity letter.

*Billy Martin's confrontations on and off the field have made him a constant headliner.*

## Blow-by-Blow with Manager Billy Martin

October 11, 1968 — Named manager of the Minnesota Twins.

August 6, 1969 — Has fistfight with Twins' pitcher Dave Boswell.

October 13, 1969 — Fired as Twins' manager, after leading team to American League West championship.

October 2, 1970 — Named manager of the Detroit Tigers.

September 2, 1973 — Fired as Tiger manager, after leading club to 1972 AL East title.

September 8, 1973 — Named manager of the Texas Rangers.

July 21, 1975 — Fired as Ranger manager.

August 2, 1975 — Named manager of the New York Yankees.

May 14, 1977 — Fined $2,500 for remarks directed at Yankee owner George Steinbrenner.

June 18, 1977 — Has dugout fistfight with Reggie Jackson.

July 24, 1978 — Resigns as Yankee manager after saying Reggie Jackson and George Steinbrenner "deserve each other. One's a born liar, the other's convicted." He alluded to Steinbrenner's plea of guilty to a charge of making an illegal contribution to President Nixon's campaign in 1972.

July 29, 1978 — Steinbrenner announces that Martin will return as Yankee manager in 1980.

November 10, 1978 — Gets into fight with Nevada sportswriter Ray Hagar.

June 18, 1979 — Replaces Bob Lemon as Yankee manager.

October 25, 1979 — Has fight with marshmallow salesman Joe Cooper.

October 29, 1979 — Fired as Yankee manager.

February 22, 1980 — Named manager of the Oakland A's.

June 1, 1981 — Suspended by the American League after bumping umpire Terry Cooney.

October 20, 1982 — Fired as A's manager.

January 11, 1983 — Hired as Yankee manager.

April 30, 1983 — Suspended for three games after kicking dirt on umpire Drew Coble.

May 25, 1983 — Has altercation with Robin Olson in a hotel bar.

June 14, 1983 — Destroys urinal in Yankee clubhouse at Cleveland Stadium.

December 4, 1983 — Fired as Yankee manager.

April 28, 1985 — Named Yankee manager, replacing Yogi Berra.

September 20, 1985 — Engages in shoving match with a bar patron in Baltimore.

September 21, 1985 — Suffers a broken arm during a fistfight with Yankee pitcher Ed Whitson.

October 27, 1985 — Replaced as Yankee manager by Lou Piniella.

### Banned Batboy

Sam Morris, a junior high school student, was enjoying his role as batboy for the Portland, Oregon, Beavers. But on the night of May 28, 1984, he wound up in the middle of an unlikely confrontation.

It began in the bottom of the 12th inning of a Pacific Coast League game between Portland and the Vancouver Canadians. Portland outfielder John Russell was ejected from the game for arguing a called third strike. Also ejected was manager Lee Elia, who hurled a metal folding chair into shallow right field.

Batboy Morris went to get the chair. "But all the Beaver players told me to stay where I was," said Morris. "The first-base umpire asked me to get it and I told her I couldn't. The Beavers pay me and I have to do what they say."

Pam Postma, the first-base umpire, then ejected the batboy.

"I've seen fans and radio announcers re-

41

moved by umpires, but never a batboy," said Elia, who played and managed in the major and minor leagues. "I thought I'd seen everything until that poor kid came into the locker room and said, 'Skip, I've been tossed out, too.' I told him not to worry about it, that it happens to everybody in baseball sooner or later."

The usual fine is about $25 for being ejected from a game, but league president William S. Cutler said Sam would not be docked.

"How do you fine a batboy?" Cutler asked.


## All in the Family

Before Ken and Bob Forsch made it to the major leagues as pitchers, there were other brother pitching combinations in baseball history — Phil and Joe Niekro, Dizzy and Paul Dean, for example.

But the Forsch brothers added a twist that will live in the record books long after them.

They were born in Sacramento, California — Ken in 1946, Bob in 1950. Both were drafted in 1968, Ken by Houston and Bob by St. Louis. While Ken was picked as a pitcher, Bob was selected as a third baseman and spent his first two professional seasons at that position.

By 1970, when he realized he couldn't hit

well enough, Bob switched to the mound. That was the year Ken began his big-league career with the Houston Astros. In 1974 Bob joined the St. Louis Cardinals.

On April 16, 1978, Bob pitched a 5-0 no-

*Ken Forsch threw his epic game as a Houston Astro.*

hitter against the Philadelphia Phillies. Then on April 7, 1979, Astro Ken threw the earliest-in-a-season no-hitter ever, beating Atlanta, 6-0.

Thus they became the only no-hit brothers in major-league history.

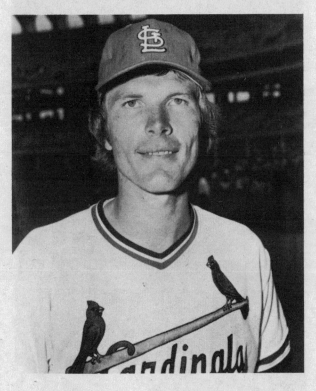

*Bob Forsch of the St. Louis Cardinals is one half of a major-league-pitching brothers act.*

# Wrigley Windfall

When the wind is blowing out at tiny Wrigley Field in Chicago, anything can happen. And the wind was definitely blowing on the afternoon of May 17, 1978, when the Phillies played the Cubs.

Four hours and three minutes after the Cubs' Dennis Lamp fired the first pitch, Steve Ontiveros grounded out to end a 10-inning game in which 45 runs were scored and 11 home runs were hit. It was the highest-scoring extra-inning game in history.

The Cubs, sparked by Dave Kingman's third homer and Bill Buckner's first (together they drove in 13 runs) tied the game at 22-22 in the eighth inning. In the tenth, the Phillies' Mike Schmidt, who had started all the scoring in the first inning with a three-run homer, hit another one to give Philadelphia a 23-22 decision. His drive came off Bruce Sutter, the eleventh pitcher in the game.

When it was over, the most relieved man in the park was Barry Foote, the Cubs' catcher. "I was so tired," he said, "I couldn't put my fingers down to give the signals."

*Dave (King Kong) Kingman hit three home runs for the Chicago Cubs in 11-homer game.*

# The Stratton Story

When they promoted him to the major leagues, the Chicago White Sox thought gangly Monty Stratton had a chance at pitching greatness. He had all the tools needed for success

*Jimmy Stewart as Monty Stratton, with June Allyson, in* The Stratton Story.

except, as events proved, luck.

In his rookie season, 1936, an appendicitis operation and tonsillectomy hampered his progress and this native of Texas finished with a 5-7 record. The next year he rolled up a 15-5 mark before a sore arm sidelined him for most of the final two months of the season. His 2.40 earned-run average was second in the league.

In 1938 his arm acted up again, but he managed to finish with a 15-9 record.

As a change of pace following that 1938 season, he was hunting rabbits on his mother's farm in Greenville, Texas. He was carrying a .22-caliber pistol in his holster and thought the gun had its safety latch on. But when he reached for the pistol, it went off. The bullet severed the large artery behind Stratton's right knee, forcing amputation of the leg.

"It was the craziest sort of accident," said Dr. A. R. Thomasson, who performed the surgery.

After the accident, Stratton was fitted with a wooden leg and spent the next three years as a White Sox coach. He then became a manager in the Class D West Texas-New Mexico League. He tried to pitch in a game but was shelled for 19 hits in nine innings.

Stratton was still determined, however, and

in 1946, pitching in the Class C East Texas League, he posted a remarkable 18-8 record. He played one more season before going to Hollywood to serve as adviser for the filming of *The Stratton Story*. Jimmy Stewart played Monty Stratton, and it was one of the best baseball movies ever made.

### Manager for a Day

It had been nine years since he last managed a major-league team. So when the Texas Rangers called, he thought it over carefully. For Eddie Stanky, it was an opportunity he thought might never come again.

After the Rangers defeated the Minnesota Twins for his first victory in June, 1977, Stanky returned to his hotel room, had a sleepless night, and realized he was a 60-year-old man whose family was more important than a job in major-league baseball. He packed his bag, called his boss, Eddie Robinson, executive vice-president of the Rangers, and said, "I quit."

Thus Stanky, who had replaced Frank Lucchesi, left a 1-0 record as Texas manager. He was temporarily replaced by Ranger third-base coach Connie Ryan.

A couple of days later, the Rangers named

Billy Hunter as manager. Within one week, the Rangers had four managers, a record that is not likely to be broken.

## Marooned in the Dome

There are 20 people in Houston who have a unique story to tell their grandchildren. They have rain checks from a game at the Astrodome.

When the massive indoor arena was first celebrated as "The Eighth Wonder of the World," the publicity had emphasized that a game never would be postponed by rain. But they can no longer make that claim because seven inches of rain flooded the Astrodome's surrounding area and prevented the umpires — and just about everybody else — from getting to the ball park for the Astros-Pittsburgh Pirates game on June 16, 1976.

"We were bone-dry inside," an Astrodome spokesman said. "The Pirates and Astros had banquet tables on the infield and sat down to dinner."

The players had arrived hours early, beating the deluge. But some 20 fans — a handful of diehards — canoed to a meal in the Astrodome cafeteria. And they pocketed their historic rain checks.

# Handyman

Cesar Tovar came out of Caracas, Venezuela, to make it to the major leagues with the Minnesota Twins in the mid-1960's. His nickname was "Pepito" and he was known as a handyman because he could play infield or outfield.

A little guy — 5-foot-7, 155 pounds — Tovar was not only adept with his glove, but was a consistent batter who had highs of .300 in 1970 and .311 in 1971.

But what he did on September 22, 1968, is why he'll be forever remembered.

On that day the Twins were playing at home against the Oakland A's. Twins manager Cal

*Cesar Tovar of the Minnesota Twins takes a fling.*

*Tovar tries another position.*

Ermer decided to tap Tovar's talents in a unique fashion. To start with, he made Tovar a pitcher — the starting pitcher. Tovar had never previously pitched in a big-league game. He gave up no hits or runs, struck out a batter, walked one, and committed a balk in the first inning.

Then he was removed as pitcher and proceeded to play one inning at each of the other eight positions. In addition to his pitching and errorless fielding, Tovar collected one hit and scored a run in the Twins' 2-1 victory.

Coincidentally, the first batter that faced Tovar on the mound was Bert Campaneris, who three years before had played all nine positions for the Kansas City A's against the California Angels.

Tovar and Campaneris are the only players in major-league history to have participated in this oddity.

# FOOTBALL

### Mystery Man

His nickname is "The Diesel" because of the way he has powered through opponents during his decade and a half with the New York Jets and Washington Redskins.

But the image of John Riggins, MVP of the Redskins' 1982 Super Bowl champions, is that of oddball or eccentric. And probably those labels are all true because of his off-the-field shenanigans.

When he was with the Jets he turned up at training camp with a Mohawk haircut. He has been known to ride halfway across the country on a motorcycle, and walk out of training camp for a day's fishing. No question he's irreverent and can be funny when he wants to. Simply, you never know what he's going to do next.

During Super Bowl Week in 1982, he showed up at a Redskin team party in top hat and tails. And when he received the MVP trophy, he attempted to unscrew the silver football from its base. Then he threatened to throw it at photographers.

He made the headlines again in the winter of 1985 at a formal National Press Club function in Washington, when he told Supreme Court Associate Justice Sandra Day O'Connor to "loosen up, Sandy, baby," and then fell asleep on the floor.

*As a New York Jet, John Riggins came to training camp with his new hairstyle.*

# Rah-rah for Okoboji and Plainfield!

Herman Richter runs a clothing store with his brother in the tiny town of Milford, Iowa, and in the early 1970's he began offering a new item for sale — University of Okoboji T-shirts.

University of Okoboji? It was a mythical institution, dreamed up by Richter, but the T-shirts caught on. And Richter realized he had a winning promotion. He expanded his line to include Okoboji pennants and car decals, and they began popping up all over the United States.

Richter named himself Okoboji's dean of student affairs and before long there actually were alumni groups in five cities, with as many as 1,000 people attending a homecoming weekend. It featured polka dancing and a marathon around Lake Okoboji (a resort north of Milford that inspired the school's name).

Okoboji's phantom football team would have been an ideal opponent for Plainfield Teachers College, which in 1941 was on its way to a record that in some respects would be unequaled.

This was the team whose scores were printed regularly in *The New York Times*, *Philadelphia Record*, *New York Post*, and other eastern newspapers. Its star was a Chinese halfback named John Chung and, according to one newspaper account, "The prowess of Chung may be due to his habit of eating rice between the halves."

The Plainfield publicity man was known as Jerry Croyden and, from all reports, things couldn't have been brighter for Chung and Plainfield. But in mid-November Croyden sent out what proved to be his last press release: "Due to flunkings in the midterm examinations, Plainfield Teachers has been forced to call off its last two scheduled games with Appalachian Tech and Harmony Teachers."

It was an abrupt finish for a team that might have been invited to one of the smaller bowl games on New Year's Day. But it was understandable in light of the story which appeared in the November 17 issue of *Time* magazine.

"For three weeks running," the account read, "the sports page of *The New York Times* has dutifully recorded the football victories of Plainfield Teachers College. . . . The only error in the reports was that Plainfield and its opponents were nonexistent."

Caswell Adams, a sportswriter on the New York *Herald Tribune*, filled in the details of the great hoax. Plainfield was dreamed up by a group of stockbrokers at Newburger, Loeb & Co., a Wall Street brokerage firm. The chief instigator was Morris Newburger, an imaginative football fan.

Newburger was Jerry Croyden. So were some of Newburger's associates. On Saturday afternoons they took turns calling the newspapers with made-up press releases.

For the stockbrokers this was certainly no money-making proposition. It was an investment in fun and fantasy. They wanted a winning football team, and they got one.

## "Mr. Square Toe"

The first thing anyone notices about Tom Dempsey is what fate decreed: He has half of a right foot and only a stub for a right hand — the results of a birth defect.

But that didn't keep him from a playing career in the National Football League.

His father encouraged the handicapped Dempsey to compete in youth athletic programs and in high school sports at Encenitas, California, where Tom played defensive end. When he arrived at Palomar Junior College in San Marcos, California, Dempsey became a kicker.

"I simply tried it one day in practice and discovered I could do it," he said.

At first he used a specially-made shoe. But

*Using his special shoe, Tom Dempsey of the New Orleans Saints kicks a record field goal.*

he discovered that he could kick higher and farther without a shoe.

Dempsey's place-kicking so impressed the New Orleans Saints, they gave him a contract in 1969. He was no longer a barefoot kicker and was able to get clearance from the NFL to use a custom-made shoe. It had no metal, the only aid being a one-and-three-quarter-inch leather boost on the "sawed-off" kicking surface.

Early in the season he drilled a 55-yard field goal against the Los Angeles Rams, one yard shy of the NFL record.

The New Orleans fans and his teammates were enthusiastic and encouraging, and he didn't mind his nicknames of "Mr. Square Toe" and "Elevator Foot."

On November 8, 1970, Dempsey kicked the field goal against the Los Angeles Rams that put him into the NFL record book. It was a 63-yarder. Nobody has been able to match it.

## Before "Hill Street Blues"

The nation's TV viewers know Ed Marinaro as an actor who used to be on *Hill Street Blues*, but college and pro football fans remember him for his role as a running back at Cornell and with the Minnesota Vikings.

As a Viking rookie he came in with a glittering reputation. At training camp the veterans invited him to join them in a card game in their dormitory. Marinaro considered the invitation as a badge of honor until he found out that he was there only to run for coffee and anything else the older guys wanted.

That first season in 1972 he drove to camp in a purple Porsche. One day Ed came out of the locker room to discover that his car had been stolen. He went down to the police station to file a report. In the midst of his filing, the news came that the car was in the middle of the Vikings' practice field.

The doors were locked. The keys were missing. Assuming that the culprits would eventually produce his keys, Marinaro left the car on the field overnight.

The next morning, as he was dressing for practice, he was informed that coach Bud Grant wanted to see him. Grant was pacing impatiently and there were about 1,000 fans waiting to watch practice when Marinaro came out.

"What is your car doing in the middle of the practice field?" the coach demanded. "What were you doing last night?"

After a lame explanation, Marinaro returned to the locker room. His keys were in his stall. Sheepishly, he dashed out on the field and, in full uniform, drove the car off the playing surface.

### Girl in the Huddle

Rarely does a September go by without a story about a girl fighting for the right to play on a high school football team.

Invariably there is strong resistance from school officials and the football coach. But in the case of Bridgette Farris, she was welcomed with open arms.

Bridgette, a soccer star at Hoover High School in Fresno, California, told football coach Pat Plummer that she thought she could make a contribution to the team. This was at the beginning of the 1985 season. Knowing that his team hadn't won a game in 1984, Plummer was willing to try anything to achieve a change in fortune. He gave Bridgette a uniform.

More than that, he waved her into a game as a placekicker on September 20 and she kicked an extra point, becoming the first girl to score a point in a high school football game in the state of California.

Coach Plummer, jubilant over Hoover's 9-0 victory over Dinuba High, credited Bridgette with being an important element in the triumph. "By her stepping out there — a hundred-pounder, a female in uniform, a high-pressure kick — and sending the first one right through, well, our guys got pumped up after that," he said.

## "The Refrigerator"

It was on ABC's Monday Night Football, so a nationwide television audience was watching Chicago play San Francisco on October 21, 1985.

William Perry, the 308-pound Bear rookie,

is a defensive tackle whose size got him the nickname "The Refrigerator" when he played at Clemson College.

With the Bears, Perry hadn't been getting much playing time because of the presence of two star veteran defensive tackles, Dan Hampton and Steve McMichael.

Two weeks earlier, when the Bears previously played the 49ers, Chicago coach Mike Ditka had put Perry in as a ball-carrier to run out the clock on the final two plays. He gained four yards.

In the Monday Night Football game, Ditka decided to try Perry again as a fullback. With the Packers leading, 7-0, Perry used his bulk as a blocking back to pave the way for a touchdown by Walter Payton.

Three minutes later, Bear quarterback Jim McMahon handed off to Perry and he barreled over from the one-yard line for the go-ahead touchdown that led to the Bears' seventh straight victory, 23-7.

The unlikely touchdown by a 300-pound-plus player produced an enormous reaction throughout the nation. One sports columnist wrote, "What Mike Ditka did with William Perry was the best use of fat since bacon."

Perry became an instant folk hero, sought for product endorsements and network tele-

"Faster! Harder!" shouts the 36-year-old coach. He blows a silver whistle attached by a band to his right wrist to signal a repeat of an exercise.

"Wake up, Brad!" he calls to one of his players. "Do it right. *Learn* from it."

Practice continues through the afternoon, with the boys taking their coach's commands with good-natured respect. As the last rays of the sun signal the end of the session, Coach Ludwig brings the squad together.

"Remember, you can do whatever you believe you can do," he says. "Don't ever take no for an answer. . . . You've got to condition yourself for the long run. Now get out there for that extra lap around the field."

As the boys do their final trot, the coach relaxes in his chair — an electric wheelchair. Seventeen years earlier, Brian Ludwig had broken his neck in a football game, shattering the fourth and fifth cervicals of his spinal cord. At the time he was a 160-pound sophomore linebacker at Bethany College. The injury left him paralyzed from the shoulders down.

Although confined to a wheelchair ever since, Ludwig has managed to fulfill his dream of becoming a teacher and coach. He is an inspiration to all who come into contact with him.

# Wild Impulse

Old coaches don't give up easily. When they retire, they still like to go to the games and follow the action. That's how it was with James Johnson, who had been head football coach at East Carolina University in Greenville, North Carolina.

On October 12, 1977, the long-retired Johnson was wearing his East Carolina cap and standing on the sidelines as his old team played William & Mary in the Oyster Bowl at Norfolk, Virginia.

With William & Mary threatening to score late in the third quarter, quarterback Tom Rozantz started off around left end, 12 yards from the end zone. He was in the clear.

But suddenly the 65-year-old Johnson darted from the sideline. He took a couple of steps, lunged, and grabbed Rozantz around the waist. "I was stunned, to say the least," Rozantz would say later. He shook off the surprising intruder and stumbled the final two yards for what proved to be the winning touchdown in William & Mary's 21-17 upset victory.

The officials led the old coach off the field. "What could I do?" he asked. "I knew he was going to score. I guess I shouldn't have done it. I'm getting too old for this."

## Twin Package

When Paul O'Connor took over as football coach at North Central College in 1985, he thought it was time to have his eyes checked. He'd never had eye problems before, but at his first practice session he was seeing double.

His eyes were okay, but he had three sets of identical twins on his squad. Actually, there were four sets of twins, but the fourth were fraternal, not identical. And to top things off, there was Dan Rickert, a linebacker who was one half of a set of twins.

*The North Central College twins, from front to back, and left to right: Don and David Ricks, Tim and Tom Franklin, Ken and Greg Wilson, and Frank and Wes Hobart.*

So the Naperville, Illinois, institution began the season with four and a half sets of twins, which stands as an all-time collegiate record until someone disproves it.

Coach O'Connor also had identification problems with twins when he was assistant coach at Southwest Missouri State. Especially difficult were Don and Dave Ricks. Don — or was it Dave? — was better at running back kickoffs.

O'Connor resolved the riddle by calling them "Punt Return Ricks" and "Kickoff Return Ricks."

## Money Isn't Everything

In an era when football coaches frequently jump from one school to another that offers more money, Lou Holtz shocked the coaching fraternity in the summer of 1985.

Holtz had had a good 1984 season at the University of Minnesota. Eighteen thousand new season tickets were sold and the university's football income had risen by about $2 million.

"Lou has been the reason for the success of the football program," said associate athletic director Holger Christensen. "We want him to know that he's appreciated."

So the school offered him a 12-percent raise in salary for the 1985–86 school year. Holtz had been making $106,000.

Holtz turned down the raise!

"My paycheck is not the most important thing," Holtz explained. "I think the raise offered me can be used to better advantage by the school."

## Lateral Movement

With less than a minute and a half remaining, Stanford scored on a field goal to lead California, 20-19, in a Pacific 10 Conference game on November 20, 1982.

On the following kickoff, California's Kevin Moen, a defensive back, took the ball at the California 45, lateraled to Richard Rodgers, who ran about 10 yards and lateraled to Dwight Garner, who then ran 20 yards. By then, there were fans streaming onto the field and impeding the Stanford defenders.

Garner then lateraled to Rodgers, and Rodgers lateraled to Marriet Ford, who then lateraled to Moen, the original receiver. Moen proceeded to weave his way to a touchdown as time ran out. It added up to an unprecedented five-lateral return and a 25-20 upset victory for California.

# The Two Faces of Bud Grant

Those who only see Bud Grant as The Great Stone Face on the sidelines know nothing of the Minnesota Vikings' coach as a practical joker.

The Viking office staff has learned to expect all sorts of pranks from him. As a naturalist and fisherman at home with wildlife, he has been known to place salamanders in desk drawers of the secretaries, and he once smuggled a rooster into the ladies' room.

On April Fool's Day, 1985, the ladies discovered the toilet seats missing and three pigeons perched above.

But the front-office staff doesn't let Grant have all the fun. Once, when he opened his office door, he found a bear cub, on loan from the local zoo.

On another occasion the women borrowed a 10-foot python from the zoo and placed it on his desk. Grant coolly wrapped the python around his neck and went about his business.

# Let Them Score

It was an NFL record the Tampa Bay Buccaneers wanted for their star running back, James Wilder. They were determined to do anything they could to achieve it.

The record was "most yards rushing and receiving in a single season"—2,244 yards, accumulated in 1984 by the Los Angeles Rams' Eric Dickerson.

Tampa Bay had one game remaining, against the New York Jets on December 16, 1984, and Wilder was within reach of Dickerson's mark.

With 1:21 left in the game, he needed 16 yards to set a new record. The Bucs were ahead, 41-21, following a Wilder touchdown. In order to get possession again, the Bucs

*Tampa Bay's James Wilder figured in a strange maneuver that many claimed brought shame to the game.*

tried three onside kicks and when that didn't work, they tried something else — they stopped playing defense.

With their cornerbacks playing off the ball, they watched the Jets complete two passes and they let Johnny Hector score easily on a run.

That got the ball back to Wilder and the Buccaneers. There was time left for three plays. The Jets, outraged more over the ethics of Tampa Bay coach John McKay than by the score, stopped Wilder for a net gain of no yards on three carries. Thus he ended up with 2,229 yards to Dickerson's 2,244.

But it all didn't end with the final whistle. The Jets blasted McKay for instructing his players to let the Jets score.

"It was a total embarrassment to the NFL," said Jets coach Joe Walton. "In my twenty-seven years as a player and coach, I've never seen anything like this."

McKay responded: "I can understand how the Jets feel, but if I hadn't tried for the record, the fans would have lynched me."

The Tampa Bay coach did not escape unscathed. After the season, Pete Rozelle, the NFL commissioner, announced he had fined McKay for his no-defense tactics. The fine was estimated to be around $5,000.

# BASKETBALL

### Akeem the Dream

He was 16 years old, playing goalie in a pickup soccer game in front of his house in Lagos, Nigeria. This was in December, 1979.

"I saw this car pull up and a guy got out to watch our game," Akeem Olajuwon recalled. "I guess it was because he saw this big, tall goaltender playing. That was me. Somebody in our game kicked the ball near him and I went to get it. He said he was the basketball coach for the Nigerian national team.

"He asked me if I'd ever played basketball before. I told him no, but he asked me to go out and eat with him. I didn't want to go. I was mad that he stopped our game."

But Richard Mills, an American who had been coaching the Nigerian basketball team, was persistent. He got Olajuwon to join him

*Akeem Olajuwon of the Houston Rockets began it all on a faraway soccer field.*

at the gym, where he gave him a basketball and told him to take a shot.

"I'd never seen anybody shoot a basketball," Olajuwon said. "I didn't know how to do it. When I shot my first free throw, I just pushed it and it didn't even hit the rim. But he showed me how to flick my wrist and I tried a few more. Then he had me stand under the basket and told me to dunk the ball. I didn't know how. So he found a chair and got on it. He jumped off the chair and dunked the ball. Then he told me to do it.

"So I got on the chair and dunked it. But he wanted me to stand on the ground. I couldn't do it."

The experiment might have ended right there, but Mills didn't give up easily.

Two years later, the 7-foot, 250-pound Olajuwon came to the United States in search of a college education. By then he'd begun to play basketball, but unlike American boys who grow up with the sport, he was a raw beanpole talent with much to learn. His parents, who own and operate a cement company in Lago, expected their son to return home after four years to join the family business.

It must have been a surprise to his family when, after a year at the University of Houston during which they heard only sketchy reports of Akeem's accomplishments, he blossomed into a hero on both sides of the Atlantic.

Almost suddenly, Akeem had become a collegiate basketball star of enormous proportions. He was named the outstanding player of the 1983 National Collegiate Athletic Association Final Four. He capped a three-year collegiate career by averaging 16.9 points and 13.7 rebounds (tops in the nation) as a junior. Then, frustrated by Houston's failure to win the title and tempted by the high stakes and opportunity to play immediately in the NBA, he signed a multimillion-dollar contract in 1984 to play with the Houston Rockets.

In his first season, 1984–85, he averaged 20.6 points a game, had 440 offensive rebounds to lead the league, finished second in shot-blocking, and his slam dunks — without the use of a chair — were something to behold.

Africa's Akeem the Dream, who'd never touched a basketball until he was 16, was now a bona fide pro living the American Dream.

### Defying the Odds

The state of Indiana has long been known as a hotbed of basketball. In recent years its most famous product has been Larry Bird of the Boston Celtics.

Bill Wanstrath never got the headlines of a
Bird. But his all-around performance at Bates-
ville High in the 1978–79 season brought him
acclaim on several counts. Although his scoring average was only 8.8 points, he averaged
8 blocked shots and 12.2 rebounds a game.

The 6-foot-7, 200-pound senior was named
honorary captain of the Indiana all-state team
and was chosen as the 1979 winner of the
"Most Courageous Award" by the United
States Basketball Writers Association.

"People don't realize how good he is," said
his coach, Roy McKamey.

Bill Wanstrath was born without a left arm.

## Elmer Shotwell: All-American

Elmer Shotwell was the ideal name for a
basketball player.

He seemed to have it all. The report on him
was that he was a six-foot guard who averaged
27 points and 12.8 rebounds a game for Gladden Corner High School in Indiana. He was
reportedly a unanimous selection for the All-
Wea Creek Conference and Class C All-State
teams.

His statistics were forwarded to a Massachusetts company that solicited players of All-
American caliber. The company promised to
screen all applicants.

The All-American receives a certificate and is listed in a book that sells for $18.95. According to the company, it sends the book to college recruiters.

There seemed little doubt about Shotwell making All-American. His certificate read: "High-School All-American. This certificate is awarded to Elmer Shotwell in recognition of outstanding ability in basketball, sportsmanship, and extracurricular activities."

There was, as it turned out, no Elmer Shotwell. Nor was there a Gladden Corner High School, an All-Wea Creek Conference, or Class C competition in the state of Indiana.

It was all the creation of Phil Miller, basketball coach at Wainwright (Indiana) High School. He wanted to emphasize that anyone — even no one — can become a High School All-American. And he was determined to show that the company was only interested in selling an $18.95 book to as many All-Americans as it could lure.

Miller first became suspicious of the offer when the company suggested he nominate up to four players from his team as potential All-Americans. "Nobody has four All-Americans," Miller said.

To prove his point, he sent in the fictional Shotwell's statistics. "I could have nominated

Charley Fastbreak with the same results,"
Miller laughed.

## Chuck Connors' Backboard Shootout

He's known for his many TV roles (among
them *The Rifleman*), but there was a time when
Chuck Connors played in the big leagues of
baseball and basketball.

He played first base in one game for the
Brooklyn Dodgers in 1949 and two years later
appeared in 66 games for the Chicago Cubs.
Before that, in 1946, Connors emerged on the
roster of the Boston Celtics, who were in the
newly formed Basketball Association of America (forerunner of the NBA).

The team's first "home" game was against
the Chicago Stags at the Boston Arena. "The
game would have been at the Boston Garden,"
Chuck said, "but there was a rodeo at the
Garden, so we were booked at the Arena."

"We were taking our warm-up shots before
the game and I threw one up — maybe I was
thirty feet out — and the next thing I knew
the glass backboard was shattered. I didn't
think I threw it that hard."

The previous summer Chuck had played
baseball for Newport News, Virginia, in the
Piedmont League. When Celtic coach Honey

Russel surveyed the backboard damage, he quipped to Chuck, "I should have left you in Newport News."

*Actor Chuck Connors was once a Boston Celtic.*

The game was delayed a half hour while someone borrowed a basket and backboard from the Boston Garden, and the Stags beat the Celtics, 57-55. The 6-foot-7 Connors couldn't recall whether he made any better shots that night, but he did play 49 games as a Celtic, averaging 4.6 points a game.

The next year, Chuck's average dropped to 3.0 for four games. He didn't break any more backboards, but he was ready to devote full time to baseball. And soon thereafter to launch a truly big-league career as an actor.

### A Rookie's Goof

Derek Harper was especially pleased to be in the NBA play-offs. He was a rookie guard out of the University of Illinois, playing for the home team Dallas Mavericks against the Los Angeles Lakers on May 6, 1984.

With 31 seconds to play, the Mavericks' Pat Cummings hooked in a basket to tie the score at 108-108 and he drew a foul from Magic Johnson. Cummings missed the free throw, but somehow teammate Harper thought he'd made it.

With 12 seconds remaining, Kareem Abdul-Jabbar missed a shot. Rolando Blackman rebounded for Dallas and tossed the ball upcourt to Dale Ellis, who flipped it to Harper. At that instant Harper may have been the only one among millions watching across the nation on television who didn't know the score.

The crowd of 17,000 at Reunion Arena kept yelling "Shoot!" Harper, oblivious to it all, kept dribbling away and backing off toward midcourt.

Dallas coach Dick Motta, whose team was out of time-outs, said, "Once I saw him backing up, I realized he didn't know the score. I wanted to go out there and tackle him."

Then the clock ran out. Harper's mental lapse gave the Lakers the opportunity to win in overtime, 122-115, for a 3-1 lead in the Western Conference semifinals.

In the locker room, Harper admitted, "Yes, I thought we were up by one. I thought Pat had made the free throw."

It was one sad night for the rookie.

### Unwanted

An advertisement was placed in several New York area newspapers in the summer of 1980. It sought applicants for the head basketball coaching job at Seton Hall University in South Orange, New Jersey. It read as follows:

## BASKETBALL — MEN'S

Head basketball coach. College exp. not req. A top-notch recruiter is what we are looking for. We suffered here in the past & this is our main priority. Duties also include coaching, scouting, dealing with top-level administrators, & public relations work. Please only conscientious hard workers need apply. Salary $28,500 plus car, plus expenses, major medical, Blue Cross, Blue Shield. No phone calls. Send resume & cover letter attn: President, Seton Hall University, South Orange, N.J. 07079.

The ad came as a surprise to Seton Hall's president, the Rev. Laurence Murphy; athletic director Richard Regan, and head basketball coach Bill Rafter. They hadn't placed the ad.

There was no vacancy and Seton Hall was happy with its coach. But a disgruntled fan or group of fans had decided to have some fun. The ad drew more than 20 responses.

Worse still, the person placing the ads had the nerve to have Seton Hall billed for them.

"The university is not going to pay for the ad," insisted Jim Lampariello, Seton Hall's promotion director.

# Playing Both Sides

Can a player play for both teams in an NBA game?

Automatically, the answer to this trivia question would be: No.

But Harvey Catchings, Ralph Simpson, and Eric Money are living proof that one can play for both teams.

It happened to them in the 1978–79 season.

On November 8, 1978, the New Jersey Nets protested the Philadelphia 76ers' 137-133 overtime victory, claiming that a referee charged the Nets' Bernard King and coach Kevin Loughery with three technical fouls, one more than the NBA permits before automatic ejection from the game.

NBA commissioner Lawrence O'Brien upheld the protest and rescheduled the game for March 23, 1979. But in the interim the Nets and 76ers made a trade which sent Simpson and Catchings to the Nets and Money to the 76ers.

The game was resumed with 5:50 remaining and the 76ers ahead, 84-81. Money scored four points for the 76ers, his new team, while Catchings tallied eight points for the Nets, his new team, as the 76ers won for a second time, 123-117.

The composite box score, showing all three

as playing for both teams, had Money with a total of 27 points and Catchings and Simpson with 8 each.

As unlikely as it seems, the same thing could happen again under similar circumstances.

## "Leaping Lizard"

As a five-year-old, Lynette Woodard watched in horror as an Air Force jet plunged from the sky into her Wichita, Kansas, neighborhood —killing 30 residents and just narrowly missing her home. Apart from the everlasting memory of the tragedy, the event would change her whole life.

*Lynette Woodard: The newest Harlem Globetrotter.*

Five years later in 1970, across the street from her house on the site of the crash, a basketball court was built. It was there at Piatt Park that Lynette became "hooked on hoop," playing pickup games daily with the neighborhood youngsters. "Soon the guys would pick me before their friends," she proudly remembered.

In high school, Lynette starred for the women's team which won state championships in 1975 and 1977, and as a coed at the University of Kansas she continued to rule the court. Though the "Leaping Lizard," as she was called, didn't get to compete in the 1980 Olympic Games because of the U.S. boycott, she did make the Olympic team. Before graduation from the University of Kansas in 1982, Lynette was elected to their Hall of Fame as the top career-scorer — man or woman — with a record 3,649 points.

In 1984, the 5-foot-11 guard seemingly topped her career by leading the U.S. Olympic basketball team to a gold medal as its captain.

Her career as a basketball player was figured to be over after the Los Angeles Olympics. Whereas Lynette's male counterparts could embark on professional careers in the NBA, there seemed to be no future in women's professional basketball.

But in the fall of 1985, twenty-six-year-old Lynette found another way to keep dribbling. The newspaper headlines said it: HARLEM GLOBE-TROTTERS SIGN A WOMAN.

The woman was Lynette Woodard. She would be the first of her sex to play for the famous Harlem Globetrotters — a team that has appeared before tens of millions, live and on television, around the globe.

## The Kid Who Shot Straight

Fourteen-year-old Craig (Clay) Schroeder fidgeted nervously as he approached the center-court stripe of Buffalo's Memorial Auditorium. This was at halftime of the NBA game in 1973 between the Buffalo Braves and the Los Angeles Lakers.

The ball players, returning to the court for second-half warm-ups, paused interestedly as Schroeder, the 80th participant in the "Dodge Colt Shootout," thought to himself, *Just get it close.*

Clay leaned back and launched a left-handed push shot. It miraculously creased the cords, to the delight of 12,730 fans and one stunned 14-year-old.

He was too young to drive, but he had just won a Dodge Colt.

"As I walked away, Wilt Chamberlain said, 'I couldn't have made it' and Gail Goodrich and Jerry West told me 'Nice shot,' " Clay recalled. "After the game I was on the radio in interviews."

The newspapers made a big thing of it, too. The Tonawanda (N.Y.) *News* knighted him with the nickname "Half-court." Another paper noted that he would be the first teenager whose father had to ask him for permission to use the car.

Clay was a freshman at Starpoint Central High School and he had no interest in pursuing a career in basketball. He was satisfied to have the best statistic of all — one-for-one from midcourt. Try and top that!

### Comeback

He was a cadet at the United States Military Academy, star of the basketball team.

Suddenly Dennis Schlitt, a 6-foot-1 guard from Milwaukee, was stricken with a rare disease, mediastinitis, an infection which started as an abcess on his neck and began to spread throughout his body.

Beginning in the spring of 1983, Schlitt underwent five operations during a two-week span. His weight dropped from 173 to 113 pounds. Twice during his stay at Walter Reed Hospital, last rites were administered.

Against all odds, Schlitt began to show improvement and after more than two months in the hospital, he returned home to Milwaukee to recuperate. He began a strength and conditioning program. Slowly he regained weight. In January 1984 he returned to classes at West Point and the doctors gave him the go-ahead to play basketball again.

"Basketball was truly a driving force for Dennis," said Jim Oxley, a former Army athlete who was the team physician. "Everybody kept telling him he'd be back playing, but they meant it only halfheartedly. That really was his goal."

Repeated surgery had left Schlitt with 75-percent lung capacity, so he wasn't able to play for long stretches at a time. He appeared in 11 of the Cadets' 29 games, averaging nearly eight minutes a game. He scored 30 points during that 1984–85 season.

"The mere fact that he went on the basketball floor and participated is beyond anyone's expectations," said his coach, Les Wothke. "He was an inspiration to all of us. He taught us one thing—never to give up hope."

His stirring comeback inspired his selection as recipient of the United States Basketball

Writers Association "Most Courageous" Award for 1985.

"What I went through I can't change," Schlitt said. "I might be marred for life, but I feel as if I can do anything."

Schlitt graduated as a 2nd Lieutenant in the U.S. Army in the summer of 1985.

## Wilt's Sweetest Night

Hershey, Pennsylvania, is known the world over as the home of the Hershey chocolate bar. But to historians of pro basketball, Hershey means something else.

It was on March 2, 1962, that the Philadelphia Warriors met the New York Knickerbockers in a regular-season NBA game at Hershey. This was considered one of Philadelphia's home games.

The star of the Warriors was a 7-foot-plus native of Philadelphia, Wilt Chamberlain. And this would be a night to remember.

Opening up with 23 points in the first quarter, Chamberlain had a total of 41 at the half and 69 before the third period had ended. In the fourth quarter, his teammates began feeding him the ball consistently in an effort to get Wilt past his own record of 78 points scored earlier in the season.

He not only broke the record, but he kept

pouring the ball through the hoop. With less than a minute left in the game, Wilt dunked a shot for his final two points. It gave him a total of 100 points for the night — a record that has never been matched.

He shot 36-for-63 from the field, 28-for-32 from the foul line. Oh, yes — the Warriors won, 169-147.

*Wilt Chamberlain after "The Game of the Century."*

# Going Batty

Big-league baseball teams periodically have bat days in which they offer free bats as an incentive to young fans.

At Fergus Falls (Minnesota) High School, they offer their own basketball version of Bat Day — live bats.

"We see them periodically in the gym throughout the winter," athletic director Don Kostelecky said. He thinks the noise and excitement of the spectators causes vibrations that drive the bats out of their hiding places and into the stands. They've swooped through the crowds, causing more than a little upset, but no bat has dunked through the basket so far.

Exterminators have tried without success to get rid of them. You can't really blame the bats. They obviously enjoy seeing the games for free.


# Skyjack

The Pepperdine College basketball team squeezed out an 89-88 victory over the University of Nevada-Reno on February 26, 1972, and boarded a Western Airlines jet for the flight home.

The team, coach Gary Colson said, was in

high spirits. That was the problem. The airline said one of the stewardesses heard a player saying that his companions were hijackers and the plane was going to be skyjacked to Florida. The stewardess reported it to the pilot as he taxied out for takeoff.

The pilot radioed the control tower and the plane taxied back to the passenger ramp — where the FBI removed the eight-man team, two coaches, and a referee who was flying with them. They were questioned for three hours and released.

While he acknowledged that skyjacking is not something that one trifles with, Colson said, without intending to pun, "The stewardess didn't have to make a federal case out of it."

## Long Ride Home

The basketball team at Colonel White High School in Dayton, Ohio, loaded up a bus for its three-hour, 150-mile trip to Toledo. Colonel White had won its first two games and was looking forward to making it three straight against Toledo's Spencer-Sharples High.

"When we pulled up to the school, there was nobody anywhere," said Colonel White coach Neal Huysman. "The school was boarded up."

It turned out that Spencer-Sharples was among 11 schools in Toledo that were closed as part of a slash in the budget.

It was a long ride home, but not as long as the one experienced by Miami University of Ohio after it defeated Toledo, 79-70, in a Mid-American Conference game in the winter of 1978.

It was snowing in blizzard proportions and the Miami team ended up spending the night in the Vandalia, Ohio, city jail. The weather got so bad, in fact, that they spent two nights there. One morning the team responded to a call for help from a Vandalia nursing home, whose staff had been on duty for 36 consecutive hours. The players shoveled snow, mopped floors, fed the residents, and even gave shaves.

## The Longest Shot

There was only one tick remaining on the Dallas Memorial Auditorium clock as the Dallas Chapperals played the Indiana Pacers on November 13, 1967. It was an American Basketball Association game and Dallas had just scored to take a 118-116 lead.

The ball was inbounded to Indiana's Jerry Harkness at his own end of the court, and with one second left he pivoted and shot just before the buzzer sounded. It traveled a record 92 feet and swished through the basket.

It was a three-point shot and enabled Indiana to win, 119-118.

"I've been practicing that shot all day," joked Harkness after the game. "There was no time to do anything except throw the ball up, so I just fired away. I didn't aim. I just let it go."

## Toothy Remarks

Larry Calton was doing play-by-play for the University of Evansville's basketball game against Pepperdine in January, 1982.

He forgot his role when he disagreed with an official's call and began to protest. The official accused Calton of not only screaming at him but of pulling his false teeth out during the argument and later challenging the Pepperdine coach to a fight.

The official slapped Calton with a technical foul. "I don't think I deserve the technical," Calton insisted. "I didn't pull my teeth out. They just fell out while I was talking and I had to push them back in."

This may have been the first time a broadcaster ever received a technical foul.

## Pro for a Day

What youngster interested in sports hasn't had dreams of one day playing in the big leagues? It could be baseball, football, basketball . . . whatever his or her favorite sport.

Even after he became a sportswriter on the Baltimore *Evening Sun*, Mike Janofski still retained boyhood fantasies—and he found a way to fulfill them.

In 1971 the 24-year-old Janofski was invited to the training camp of the NBA's Baltimore Bullets. It was all by prearrangement. He would write a rookie diary for his newspaper.

Janofski was a 6-foot-1 guard out of the University of Maryland. He'd grown up with a basketball, but playing in the pros? He'd soon find out.

On September 25, the Bullets were playing an inter-league exhibition game at Greensboro, North Carolina, against the Carolina Cougars of the American Basketball Association. There was 1:21 left in the game when Baltimore coach Gene Shue looked down his bench and signaled Janofsky to go into the game.

"Entering the game," the public address announcer began, "is Mike Janofsky, No. 23. He's also a sportswriter for the Baltimore *Evening Sun*."

The crowd was at first confused, then amused, when Mike fouled Carolina's Larry Miller. Then he intentionally fouled Gene Littles, who hit two free throws.

Mike's professional debut was going nowhere until, after a time-out, he took a pass and arched a 20-foot jump shot over Littles. The ball banked off the backboard and through the net.

The crowd gave Mike a standing ovation. The game ended without Mike getting off another shot. He retired forever with a 1,000 field-goal percentage.

And went back to the typewriter.

## Clown Night

It was Clown Night at Rice University, where the Rice cagers were playing Texas on February 7, 1978.

Many fans wore floppy shoes, noses that looked like red tomatoes, fright wigs, and plastic hats.

The idea was suggested by Texas coach Abe Lemons after Rice coach Mike Schuler had made 99 substitutions in the previous meeting of the teams. Lemons said then that all Rice needed were clowns to make the game a circus.

Indeed, it turned out to be a circus of sorts.

Going into the final quarter, the game was close until Rice's Alan Miller fouled Tyrone Branyan as Branyan made a layup. When referee Joe Shoshid called it an intentional (two shots) foul, Rice's Schuler jumped to his feet and started yelling. He was hit with two technicals.

Branyan sank two free throws, Jim Krivacs sank four more free throws (two for each technical), and then Texas took the ball out of bounds and scored the ninth and tenth straight points on a Branyan layup. It amounted to a 10-point play.

Texas wound up winning the game, 102-86, and Coach Lemons said he enjoyed the circus.

## Surprise for the Globetrotters

Despite their "showboating" — their hidden-ball tricks, their pepper games, their hilarious arguments with the referees — the Harlem Globetrotters rarely lose a game.

While clowning, they're serious enough to want to win and their attitude was no different when they took the floor against Seattle University in Seattle on January 21, 1952.

The Globies usually don't play college teams, but this was a special game designed to bring money to the Olympic Games fund. The Trot-

*Seattle University's Johnny O'Brien is on his way to a field goal against the Harlem Globetrotters.*

ters were donating their services.

The best of the Trotters was Goose Tatum. Nobody was bigger than 6-foot-4 on the Seattle team, which featured the 5-foot-9 O'Brien twins, Eddie and Johnny. Johnny was among the nation's leading scorers.

The college boys got off to an early lead and there was less and less clowning by the Trotters as Seattle led, 46-36, at half.

The Trotters came back to take a 55-54 lead but they were behind again, 65-59, at the end of the third quarter. In the final period, the Trotters closed the gap, but Johnny O'Brien, playing the game of his life, made the difference. He scored a total of 43 points and Seattle surprised the Trotters, 84-81.

Did the O'Brien twins go on to greater feats in basketball? No.

What they did do was more amazing than the night they took the Trotters. Eddie and Johnny O'Brien became major-league baseball players with the Pittsburgh Pirates—a twin combination at shortstop and second base.

*Gordie Howe & Sons as Hartford Whalers: (left to right) Marty, Gordie, Mark.*

# HOCKEY

## The Ageless Gordie Howe

Nobody could argue the description of Gordie Howe as the most durable player in the history of pro hockey.

He was a 6-foot, 200-pound right wing from the wheat fields of Saskatchewan who started his career with the Detroit Red Wings in 1946 at the age of 18.

He was hailed as a seemingly indestructible man of steel. Howe's career — and his life — were almost snuffed out in his third season with the Red Wings. He collided with Toronto's Ted Kennedy during a 1950 Stanley Cup play-off game, crashed head-on into the sideboards, and suffered severe brain injury. He hovered between life and death while surgeons operated to relieve pressure on the brain.

Howe recovered to become, as Montreal's famed Jean Beliveau said, "the best hockey player I have ever seen."

He ended a 25-year career with the Red Wings in 1971 and everyone presumed his skates were hung up forever. But in 1973, at the age of 45, he made a historic return to play with his sons Marty and Mark for Houston in the World Hockey Association. In 1977 Howe and sons joined the Hartford Whalers, and Howe didn't finally retire until he played 80 games in the 1979–80 season.

He was 52 years old.

## Miracle on Ice

Although Americans are gradually making their imprint, professional hockey remains dominated by players from Canada, where the sport began on frozen ponds in the eastern provinces of Quebec and Ontario. It figured that as a nation Canada would lead the way in the Olympic Games as well.

Indeed, starting with the Games of 1920, Canada won the gold medal in six of the first seven competitions. Russia became a powerful force in 1956 when it was first. But in 1960 the U.S. surprised the world by winning gold for the first time at Squaw Valley, California.

The Soviets came back to capture the next four Olympics, and then came the 1984 Games at Lake Placid, New York. The U.S. was coached by Herb Brooks, known for his demanding, disciplined routine and organizational skills. The team played a grinding 62-game exhibition schedule and it learned the aggressive European style. It was considered the best prepared of any hockey squad that had ever represented the U.S. in international competition.

But only dreamers could even whisper of a gold medal for this collection of collegians and minor-league players whose average age of 22 made them the youngest squad in the Olympics. The Russians were clear-cut favorites. After all, they'd beaten a National Hockey League All-Star team, 6-0, the previous year, and only a couple of days before the start of the 1980 Olympics, the Soviets had crushed the U.S., 10-3, in an exhibition game.

In the preliminary round, the U.S. scored comeback victories over Sweden and Czechoslovakia, and it continued undefeated by beating Norway, Romania, and West Germany. Meanwhile, Russia also won all five of its games.

This set the stage for a final-round meeting

between the U.S. and Russia on February 22, 1980, George Washington's birthday. Three times the Russians led, but goals by Mark Johnson and Mike Eruzione gave the U.S. a history-making 4-3 victory. And the players sang "God Bless America."

But they still had to play for the championship against Finland. Trailing, 2-1, entering the final period, the U.S. tied the game on a goal by Phil Verchota. Two more goals by Rob McClanahan and Mark Johnson enabled the U.S. to clinch, 4-2, the gold medal.

The newspaper headlines called it "A Miracle on Ice."

## A Ref's Vision

Referees, or umpires, in every sport are constantly hooted by fans — and players — who call them "blind" when a decision goes against their favorite team.

Bill Chadwick typically experienced his share of such criticism when he refereed in the National Hockey League. He was an American, a rarity, in what was essentially a Canadian game.

He was known for refusing to give in to pressure from players, club officials, or fans. He was recognized as one of the leading referees and this is reflected in his having been assigned to a record 105 Stanley Cup play-off games.

As an amateur player, Chadwick had suffered a freak accident when a stray puck struck him in the eye. He continued to play hockey and later took up his career as a referee.

What few people knew about Chadwick was that when they called him blind, they were half right. As a result of his accident, he had lost the sight in his right eye.

## Sutter Sextet

They grew up on a 640-acre farm in Alberta, Canada — a working farm of wheat and oats, pigs and cattle, fruits and vegetables.

They walk into the IGA supermarket in their hometown of Viking, where their mother works part-time at a checkout counter, and heads turn and people murmur. They produce the same head-turning and whispers when they enter a restaurant on Long Island or in Chicago or St. Louis or Philadelphia — their main centers of employment.

They are the Sutter brothers—hockey's first family. If they were a circus act, they would be billed as "the daring, death-defying, dynamic Sutters."

In hockey circles they are recognized simply as The Sutters.

There are six of them — yes, six — playing in the National Hockey League: Brian, left wing, St. Louis Blues; Darryl, left wing, Chicago Black Hawks; Duane, right wing, New York Islanders; Brent, center, New York Islanders; Richie, right wing, Philadelphia Flyers; and Ron, center, Philadelphia Flyers.

There is another Sutter brother, Gary, the oldest at 30, who played amateur hockey and became a coach. The youngest, Richie and Ron, are twins.

There have been other famous brothers in hockey — Maurice and Henri Richard; Doug and Max Bentley; and Frank, George, Billy, and Bob Boucher. The Bouchers had the most brothers — four — until the "daring, death-defying, dynamic Sutters" came off the farm.

### Get In There and Fight!

Coaches dating back to the earliest days in sports have encouraged their players to "never give up without a fight."

But they don't mean it literally. They exhort you to play hard, give it all you've got, match brawn with brawn. That's how you fight.

This was not the case, however, on January

24, 1982, when the Los Angeles Kings played the Vancouver Canucks in a National Hockey League game.

At one point in the game a fight developed between Ron Delorme of Vancouver and a Los Angeles player. Delorme was sent to the penalty box, but before his penalty had expired, he jumped out of the box and started a fight.

Sitting on the Los Angeles bench was Paul Mulvey, a 23-year-old left wing. Kings coach Don Perry turned to Mulvey and ordered him to leave the bench and join the fight. Mulvey refused.

"I'm a human being and I stuck up for my rights as a person," Mulvey said. "I was being shoved out there as if I was nothing, with no respect for my hockey ability at all. I'm not going to be a designated assassin. . . . If that's the only thing I can do in the NHL, go out and fight, then maybe my career is over."

A week later Mulvey was shipped out to New Haven of the American Hockey League. A grievance on his behalf was filed by the NHL Players Association. NHL president John Ziegler responded by suspending Coach Perry for 15 days and fining the Kings $5,000.

"I believe the actions of the coach did not and do not reflect the policy or attitude of the Los Angeles hockey club," Ziegler said.

"Nevertheless, the club must be held account-able for the conduct of its employees."

### Shell-Shocked Goalie

"You don't feel anything. It's like a tornado, it happens so fast."

Michel Dion, the Pittsburgh Penguins' goalie, was referring to his experience in a game against the New York Islanders on January 26, 1982.

*Michel Dion of the Pittsburgh Penguins has had better nights than the explosive one against the New York Islanders.*

Just one minute and 31 seconds into the game, Duane Sutter put the Islanders ahead. About a minute later, John Tonelli made it 2-0. Then Bryan Trottier scored twice in 45 seconds, followed by Sutter's second goal at 4:08 to give the Islanders a 5-0 lead.

Although the NHL doesn't keep this specific record, the Islanders' five goals were believed to be the largest number ever scored in so short a time span from the start of a game.

The shell-shocked Dion, a quality goalie who the following day was named a starter in the league's All-Star Game, was removed from the game after the fifth tally and the Islanders went on to win, 9-2.

### Ill-Fated Hero

Bill Barilko never really seemed destined for fame. Only 19 when the Toronto Maple Leafs called him up from the minors at the end of the NHL's 1946–47 season, the 190-pound defenseman quickly established himself as a defensive defenseman — the kind who doesn't score goals, doesn't make all-star teams, and doesn't get his picture in the papers very often.

But, while he wasn't a star, Barilko was no slouch, either, and in each of his first three seasons he played an important role as the Maple Leafs won the Stanley Cup. The Leafs lost in the first round of the 1950 play-offs, but were back in the finals in 1951 against the Montreal Canadiens.

Barilko was a key figure in the first game when he dived to block a Maurice Richard shot headed for an open net. It preserved a 2-2 tie and Toronto went on to win in sudden-death overtime.

Montreal won the next game, but Toronto took the next two, both again in overtime. The Leafs returned to a joyous greeting at Maple Gardens as they prepared to clinch the Cup in the fifth game on April 21, 1951. For the first time in the series it didn't look as if the game would go into overtime. With a minute to go, Montreal held a 2-1 lead. But the Leafs got a goal with 32 seconds left to force the game into overtime.

After only 2:53, it was sudden death for the Canadiens when Barilko took a pass at mid-ice and in blind desperation fired a shot that skipped past the Montreal goalie. The Stanley Cup had returned to Toronto, and Barilko, the usually unsung player, was a hero at last.

After the season, he went home to Timmons, a mining town in northern Ontario. In August he and a friend, Dr. Henry Hudson, flew into northern Canada on a fishing trip in the doctor's private plane. They were never heard from again.

## Long Night

They were playing in an arena famous as the site where the United States hockey team won the Olympic gold medal in 1980.

The ultimate for Bowling Green and Minnesota-Duluth was to capture the 1984 National Collegiate Athletic Association championship on March 24 in Lake Placid, New York.

Their coaches had promised them it wouldn't be easy. When it was over, the players slumped from exhaustion.

They had skated 97 minutes and 11 seconds of game time, nearly four hours on the clock. The teams had been tied, 4-4, at the end of regulation time and it didn't end until Bowling Green's Gino Cavallini scored the sudden-death goal for a 5-4 victory in the fourth overtime period.

It was the longest and most memorable game in NCAA tournament history.

# GOLF

## Holes-In-One

For golfers there is no single feat more exciting than making a hole-in-one. It doesn't happen very often.

Jim Cobb, a 69-year-old golfer from Craig, Colorado, wonders what all the fuss is about.

On August 4, 1985, he sank a 7-iron shot on the 167-yard seventh hole at the Meeker Golf Course. The next day, at Yampa Valley, he holed a 5-iron shot on the 167-yard third hole and aced the 162-yard ninth hole with a 4-iron.

Three holes-in-one in less than 30 hours!

Cobb, who is semiretired, conceded that luck could have been a factor, but said skill came into play, too.

"They weren't fluke shots. . . . They were real good swings all three times," he said.

## Bull's-Eye

Doug Sanders, who was one of the leading professional golfers, welcomed the chance to play in a foursome that included comedian Bob Hope, Senator George Murphy of California, and Spiro Agnew, Vice-President of the United States.

They were playing in the Bob Hope Classic, a charity tournament, on February 7, 1970, in Palm Springs, California. Agnew was a sub for President Richard Nixon, whose White House duties kept him from participating.

This distinguished foursome had drawn dozens of photographers who were focusing on the Vice-President, whose drive off the first tee had landed in the rough.

Sanders was standing in the middle of the fairway near Hope's electric cart when Agnew hit an iron shot out of the rough. It hit Sanders in the left side of the head.

Sanders rubbed his head in disbelief. The blow drew blood. The Vice-President rushed over and apologized.

After being treated by a doctor, Sanders finished the round with his foursome. A discouraged Agnew later hit a wood shot right into the crowd of spectators and remarked, "I'm going to kill somebody."

"That's all right," Hope quipped to Agnew. "You keep the gallery on its toes. Not everybody gets hit by a Vice-President."

# RUNNING

### Zola Budd's Secret Race

Eighteen-year-old Zola Budd made headlines during the 1984 Olympics as the barefoot South African who cost America's Mary Decker her chance of a gold medal in the 3,000-meter race.

Many, including Decker, blamed Budd for the collision that caused Decker to drop out of the race. Budd wound up seventh and gained notoriety she didn't seek. Tapes of the race showed that the collision wasn't anyone's fault and that Decker, if anyone, could have avoided it.

Just as those headlines began to fade from memory, Budd had another cross to bear — that of coming from apartheid in South Africa. Her bid to win the English cross-country title in February 1985 ended when a protester ran onto the track and forced her off the course. In July another activist tried the same interference at a race in Edinburgh, Scotland. The following week it took a cordon of police and security guards to protect her as she won a race in Birmingham, England.

On August 26, the harassed runner, now a naturalized Briton but still fearing political protest, tried a new approach. She secretly entered the 5,000-meter race at London's Crystal Palace track. That is, the promoters of the race kept it a secret.

But once she was at the starting mark, the secret was out. There were no protesters in sight as Budd shaved more than 10 seconds off the women's world record with a clocking of 14 minutes, 48.07 seconds.

## Did She or Didn't She?

"Jackie, Jackie," shouted the crowd in the streets in front of the glass-walled Prudential Tower in Boston. But those closest to the finish line at the 84th annual Boston Marathon on April 21, 1980, were confused by what they were witnessing.

The runner breasting the tape and wearing No. W50 was not the favored Jackie Gareau, who was still two minutes behind, but a runner unknown to the officials and onlookers.

"Who is she?" echoed through the milling crowd.

When Will Cloney, race director for the Boston Marathon, put the winner's crown on the young lady before him, he, too, was puzzled. She was Rosie Ruiz, a Cuban-born 26-year-old who had, according to her entry, run in only one other marathon — the New York Marathon.

Rosie's winning time was 2:34:28, 22 minutes faster than her listed New York qualifying time. Moreover, she looked fresh and rested after the 26-mile run. In the post-race interviews she gave confused, unconvincing answers about her performance and training. Explaining her unbelievable time, she simply said: "I awakened full of energy this morning."

Serge Arsenault, race director of the Montreal Marathon and a close friend of second-place finisher Jackie Gareau, said: "When I saw this woman come through in first place — and noticed how well she looked physically — I thought it was a joke."

Reporters along the race route could not recall seeing any signs of a runner wearing W50. Two witnesses from Harvard said they saw Rosie join the race a half mile before the finish line.

Subsequently, Susan Morrow, a New York photographer, claimed that she'd seen "that woman" riding a subway during the New York Marathon, the race in which Rosie supposedly qualified for Boston.

Now the sponsors of the New York Marathon got into the act. They reviewed film clips of the finish of their race and there was no sign of Rosie Ruiz finishing with a 2:56 clocking, the time she'd listed on her Boston entry.

Boston officials did a thorough investigation and found that they could not confirm that Rosie had run the entire race. They requested return of her first-place medal.

Rosie never returned the medal, but her name was stricken from the records and Jacqueline Gareau of Montreal became the official winner.

## Running Against Custom

There was no hint of the unusual when the starter signaled the beginning of the sixty-ninth Boston Marathon in 1967. Run over a 26-mile, 385-yard course between Hopkinton and Boston, Massachusetts, it was the oldest and then-largest marathon in the United States, where more than 100,000 spectators lined the course.

Suddenly, the crowd was startled to see Will Cloney, director of the race, chasing after one of the contestants. His target, K. Switzer, was to say later, "I was crying like a maniac. I was being spun around by the shoulder. . . ." Actually, Cloney was trying to rip the number off Switzer's shirt and chase the runner off the course.

But the 21-year-old Syracuse University student, eluding the official, managed to continue and finish the race, marking the start of something much bigger than that one competition. K. Switzer, it turned out, was a woman who had made a daring entry into the traditionally all-male marathon, Kathrine Switzer had filled in her entry blank simply as K. Switzer, leading officials to assume she was male.

Such was the gravity of her boldness that the AAU officially barred women from all competition with men in these long-distance events. It took a long, hard, five-year battle for the barrier to be dropped, and in 1972 women were allowed to compete with the men in the same race. A year later, a separate division was established for women competing in the Boston Marathon, and by 1984 the ultimate was achieved when women ran the marathon for the first time at the Los Angeles Olympics.

# BOXING

## Belated Revenge

Both heavyweights were attempting comebacks after lengthy absences from the ring. They were in a rematch in what was billed as "Charlotte's greatest fight" on December 14, 1977, in Charlotte, North Carolina.

It was 51-year-old Neil Wallace vs. 49-year-old Waban (Tugboat) Thomas. Thomas had twice beaten the shorter Wallace in 1957, the last time Wallace had fought. Thomas hadn't fought since the late 1960's.

This time Wallace got his revenge. He stopped Thomas in eight rounds on a technical knockout. Now it was time for these aging fighters to hang up their gloves for good.

## Biting Blow

Junior welterweights Rick Dawson and George Burton were in a close bout at Steelworkers Hall in Baltimore on March 28, 1984.

Dawson appeared to be ahead on points in the third round and he had just landed the heaviest punch of the match — a solid right to Burton's nose. They went into a clinch and referee Larry Barrett attempted to separate them.

Then Dawson bit Burton on the shoulder. Biting is okay in professional wrestling, but not in boxing. The referee disqualified Dawson as the crowd booed the sudden end to the match.

# HORSE RACING

### Jockey With Nine Lives

The young jockey accepted the award for the Philadelphia Sports Writers Association's Most Courageous Athlete of 1973. The denial in the acceptance speech carried through the dining room.

"I don't think I'm all that courageous," said the recipient. "I ride for the same reasons all jockeys do, to make a living. I ride because I love horses and not because I'm tough or brave."

But hardly any one of the 1,000 male diners at the awards dinner could believe these words. Mary Bacon, the beautiful 23-year-old woman standing before them, had just wound up another year of fierce riding in the dangerous, competitive business of thoroughbred racing, and everyone there knew how much courage that took for the female jockey.

*Mary Bacon: A symbol of courage at the racetrack.*

Mary held a track record for catastrophies. In 1969, after being thrown by a horse in Oklahoma, the 5-foot-4 jockey was hospitalized with a broken back. The resulting pinched nerves left her paralyzed from the waist down for four days.

"I'll never forget lying there and trying so desperately to wiggle my toes," she recalled. "At times like that you think a lot about how short life is, and how you'd better make the most of your chances."

So back to the track she went with less than

six weeks recovery time. One day after some hard riding in three consecutive races, she felt too ill to continue (two more races had been scheduled). After a quick call to her doctor, Mary admitted herself to the hospital, where her daughter Suzy was born several hours later. She had been riding while nine months pregnant!

In 1971, at Ellis Park in Owensburg, Kentucky, another fall from her horse resulted in a broken collarbone, leg contusions, bruised ribs, and internal bleeding. Yet 13 days later, Mary rode again.

The following year she was thrown from her mount in a Pittsburgh race. This time another horse fell on top of her. She was unconscious for six days. Five days later, she left the hospital and headed straight for the track. She rode three races, winning one and placing third in another. "You can't quit because you've been thrown," Mary said.

Being a woman racing against men made the going rougher for this beautiful young jockey. "From the moment that the starting gate opens until my horse hits the wire, I'm a man competing against men," she reasoned. But this shapely athlete who was once a *Playboy* pinup was no man by any standard. And she didn't have to put on an act to prove she was tough. All she had to do was win.

And win she did. Once she and jockey Joan Phipps were the winners of the Daily Double at New York's Aqueduct race track — a first for women jockeys. It was a sure bet that broken bones could never break the spirit of the indomitable Mary Bacon.

### Golden Goof

Ray Gallegos sells tickets to bettors at Gulfstream Park, a racetrack in Florida. He is known as a pari-mutuels clerk.

On March 10, 1984, as the horses were going into the gate for the last race, an unidentified man stepped up to Gallegos' window and ordered a $10 trifecta wheel ticket with the No. 4 horse, Arrowood Dream, on top combined with every other horse in the race.

To win a trifecta, the bettor must select the first three horses to finish in exact order.

In punching in the amount of the bet ($10), Gallegos accidentally hit the 0 button twice. A $10 trifecta wheel, with 12 horses in the race, costs $1,100. But he had made it a $100 wheel costing $11,000.

He hit the release button, the ticket came out, and when the bettor saw the total bet of $11,000, he understandably refused it.

A mutuels clerk is responsible for the amount of any error he makes when a customer refuses a ticket. Gallegos desperately tried to cancel the ticket, but he was too late. The race was underway. He called his supervisor in a panic, but there was nothing the supervisor could do. The machines were locked.

Suddenly Gallegos had become a bettor in debt to Gulfstream Park for $11,000.

The next two minutes were pure agony for Gallegos, who was facing financial ruin.

But the favored Arrowood Dream came through to win the race and Gallegos ended up a trifecta winner. Since a trifecta wheel ticket gives the buyer every possible second- and third-place combination with the chosen first-place horse, Gallegos couldn't lose.

With a trifecta payoff of $876.60 for $2, Gallegos collected $43,830 with his $100 wheel ticket. He netted $24,064 profit after paying the track $11,000 for the bet and the 20-percent income tax of $8,766.

It was the biggest mistake made by a mutuels clerk that anyone could remember. "When this sort of thing happens, the clerk almost never wins," said mutuels manager Pat Mahoney. "In this case, the poor guy would have been an eternity trying to pay it back."

# Beware the Duck!

Jockey Robert Louis Stevenson was riding Smokey Johnson in an exercise session at Florida's Gulfstream Park. Suddenly a duck ran between the horse's legs. The horse reared up, spilling the jockey.

Stevenson suffered a broken kneecap that had an adverse effect on his riding career, Stevenson's attorney charged in a lawsuit against Gulfstream.

Robert Duval, Stevenson's attorney, claimed that the duck belonged to a horse trainer and that "it is against racing commission rules to have a domesticated animal around the stable area."

The duck, apparently advised of his rights, failed to appear at a court hearing as a witness. He flew the coop. And racing odds are that he'll never be seen again.

# Call Me Buckie

In 1983 Call Me Buckie went to see a doctor — well, a veterinarian. Call Me Buckie is a show horse — that is, he competes in horse shows. But this nine-year-old gelding had been having fainting spells and his owner brought him to the University of Pennsylvania's veterinary hospital. He was diagnosed as having a heart blockage.

In humans this would call for a pacemaker, an emergency device for stimulating the heart. Why not one for Call Me Buckie? Indeed, the vets inserted a pacemaker, the first ever in a horse. It saved his life, but he couldn't do more than walk.

The widow of a horse lover, hearing of the horse's condition, donated her late husband's ultramodern pacemaker as a replacement and now Call Me Buckie can trot, canter, and jump hedges.

If he could talk, he'd say, "Call Me Lucky."

# OLYMPIC GAMES

### Wrestling Gold

When young Jeff Blatnick was a sophomore wrestler at Nisakayuna High School in a suburb of Schenectady, New York, a freshman bass player used to look up to him.

"You'd pick me up and twirl me and scare me to death," the young man later wrote Jeff. "I like to think that I was the first of many victims of your wrestling talents."

For Jeff did indeed became a talented wrestler. After graduation from high school in 1976, he went on to major in physical education at Springfield College in Massachusetts. Tragedy struck the Blatnick family in 1977 when Jeff's brother, Dave, was killed in a motorcycle accident. But the Blatnicks were a courageous family and Jeff didn't swerve from his objectives: a college degree and a Greco-Roman

*Wrestler Jeff Blatnick experiences the ultimate moment at the 1984 Olympic Games.*

wrestling berth on the 1980 Olympic team. He achieved both, but alas, for all those dedicated athletes who made the team, the United States boycotted the Games. Jeff and his fellow Americans never got to Moscow.

Jeff went on with his life and kept his sights on training for the 1984 Olympics. But in 1982 it was discovered that Jeff had Hodgkin's disease, a form of lymphatic cancer that often proves fatal.

After five days in the hospital following surgery for removal of his appendix and spleen, Jeff went home to fight the dreaded disease.

Follow-up radiation treatments and intense pain sapped him of weight and energy. He was so nauseous that he often had to leave his job as a welder and go home to suffer silently in his room. It took seven months before Jeff could finally find the strength to wrestle again. He always had the desire.

"I had this dream and I didn't let go," he said.

With the support of his family, friends, and his boss at the plant, Jeff forged ahead to make up for lost time. And make it he did — to the Los Angeles Olympics, where he competed as a 6-foot-2, 248-pounder in the heavyweight class. That in itself was a triumph, but Jeff Blatnick did not stop there. During the Games, he lost one match to a Greek wrestler who bit his wrist and drew blood. "The referee didn't call anything," said Blatnick. "I guess he thought I bit myself."

The Greek lost his next round-robin match and Jeff made it to the finals. On August 2, 1984, the 27-year-old Blatnick decisioned Sweden's Thomas Johansson to win the gold medal.

Jeff stood proudly on the podium as the medal was slipped over his head. His eyes filled with tears as he joined in the singing of "The Star-Spangled Banner."

"The last time I saw him cry was when his brother died," his mother said. "And I've never heard him sing before."

## Oldest Olympic Medal Winner

Anders Haugen was one of America's earliest ski-jumpers. As a 36-year-old Californian, he competed in the first Olympic Games in 1924 in Chamonix, France.

In the jumping competition the judges credited him with fourth place, meaning he came close but didn't get a medal. And with each Olympics since then, American jumpers have returned empty-handed.

But in 1980, at a Norwegian ski team reunion, two-time silver medalist Thorlaf Stromstad of Norway was studying the scores of the '24 Games. He found an error. The bronze medal for third place had been mistakenly awarded. The correct third-place recipient should have been America's Haugen.

Stromstad reported his findings to the International Olympic Committee and 50 years after Haugen had competed at Chamonix, he received his bronze medal. He was 86 years old, the oldest Olympian in history to earn a medal.

# A MIXED BAG

### Channeling One's Love

After four hours of swimming en route across the English Channel, Peter Johnson paused long enough to say, "Will you marry me?" to Julia Hughbanks. She was riding in the escort boat on August 13, 1985.

Julia, like Johnson, a geologist from Texas, nodded happily and the 26-year-old Johnson picked up his stroke as he continued the 21-mile swim from Cap Gris Nez, France, to St. Margaret's Bay, near Dover, England.

It took Johnson 8 hours and 20 minutes, which trimmed 14 minutes off the previous France-to-England record for the crossing. And it marked the first time a Channel swimmer ever became engaged along the way.

## Weary Booters

Simon Fraser University of Canada and Quincy College of Illinois were competing in the semifinals of the 1976 NAIA soccer championships at the Rose Bowl in Pasadena, California.

They'd met the year before in the title game, won by Quincy, 1-0. And this rematch proved just as close, but it took a lot longer.

The game started at 8:30 P.M., and at the end of regulation time the score was 1-1. One overtime led to another. Nobody could score. Now it was getting close to 1 A.M., the Pasadena curfew that could postpone completion of the game until the morning.

The teams were in their 14th overtime period when Simon Fraser's Brad Mason scored the winning goal five minutes before curfew. It was the longest collegiate soccer game ever played.

Simon Fraser went on to defeat Rockhurst, 1-0, for the championship, but the marathon game is the one the booting world will always remember.

## Grossly Exaggerated

After more than 40 years as sports information director at Duke University, Ted Mann retired in the early 1980's. From the various athletes and newspapermen he'd known over the years, there came tons of tributes for a job well done. And he was named to the North Carolina Sports Hall of Fame.

He moved to Holden Beach, North Carolina, and contented himself with following the various sports on television and reading the newspapers.

One morning he was thumbing through the pages of the weekly Brunswick *Beacon* when he suddenly let out a shriek. In cold type there was a column on the deceased Ted Mann, entitled "A Final Tribute to Ted Mann." Not some other Ted Mann, but the very Ted Mann who was reading it.

Under similar circumstances, Samuel Clemens (Mark Twain) once responded, "The report of my death has been grossly exaggerated."

A close friend of Mann's said: "He didn't think it was a laughing matter then, and he hasn't laughed yet."

The error was traced to a part-time sports reporter for the *Beacon.* He said he was told of Mann's death by a rescue squad worker. According to one version, someone called Mann's residence to check out the death report. Whoever answered said, "Mr. Mann's not here. He's gone." The caller took that to mean Mann had died.

The reporter apologized and his editor, Ed Sweatt, said, "We made the boo-boo of all boo-boos. You don't bury somebody before they're dead."

## A Whale of a Sailor

When Noel Robins was a teenager growing up in Australia, he was an excellent soccer and hockey player and he loved to race his sailboat in the waters near his home.

But when he was 21 he was involved in an auto accident that would change the course of his life. His neck was broken and he became a quadriplegic — losing the use of both arms and legs.

After years of difficult exercise and physical therapy, Robins managed to come back from his almost-total disability. He walked with a limp and a shuffle but he had full use of one arm.

Nonetheless, he was able to return to the one sport, sailing, in which he could handle his handicaps. Robins was able to steer with his one good arm — the left one — and on deck he could hold onto something to keep his balance.

His sailing skills were such that he became Australia's national Soling champion in 1977, but something bigger was still ahead. Australia was challenging the United States for the America's Cup, the most coveted prize in international yachting. Robins was chosen as skipper over Australia's leading sailor, Olympic gold medalist David Forbes.

That in itself was a towering triumph for Robins: helmsman of the 12-meter *Australia*. In the America's Cup races, his counterpart aboard America's *Courageous* was the celebrated Ted Turner, owner of television networks, the Atlanta Braves, and the Atlanta Hawks. And one fine sailor.

They had their confrontation in the waters off Newport, Rhode Island, in the fall of 1977. The perfect ending would have Robins and *Australia* wresting the America's Cup from the U.S. It didn't happen that way. The U.S. swept the first four races in the best-of-seven series.

Robins and his crew and countrymen were, of course, disappointed. But there was no shame in losing to a country that had repelled every challenge since 1870. And the remarkable Robins had experienced the ultimate in sailing competition — something he never could have imagined at the time of his auto accident 20 years earlier.

In 1983, the Cup finally went Down Under when Australia defeated the United States.

## Skirting the Issue

Girls playing Little League baseball? Football? Ice hockey? Never, it was once said. Yet, today, thanks to the changes in law (Title IX) girls can compete in every sport boys do and it's not unusual, although still resisted by traditional jocks, to find girls playing alongside boys in contact sports.

The same law, of course, protects boys in the reverse way and at the start of the 1985 school year at Northampton High School in Massachusetts, five male seniors made the girls' varsity field hockey team.

"We think it's really cool having guys on the team," admitted 16-year-old co-captain Victoria Stone.

The boys, however, have to keep their sights on the essentials of the sport, since they're newcomers to the traditional all-girl activity.

"We just try to concentrate on the game," said 17-year-old Richard Pushkin. "The girls are much better than the boys."

And according to the letter of the law, the

boys are treated exactly the same as the girls. The only difference, however, is that they have their own locker room. Even the uniform, which the boys voted on, is the same — including the blue, yellow, and white plaid kilt.

"We thought it was great when they decided to wear the skirts," commented co-captain Deborah Mansfield. "It would have made them [the boys] stand out if they had worn shorts."

But principal Dr. Gordon Noseworthy, usually a strong advocate of coed education, still had some doubts.

"Boys in skirts, playing a traditional girls' sport — that's heady stuff," he said.

### Eyewitness

Joe Walker rarely misses the games of the Atlanta Hawks, the Atlanta Falcons, and the Atlanta Braves.

As sports director of WAOK(AM) and V103(FM), and columnist for the weekly Atlanta *Voice*, he follows the action at courtside or from the press box and does interviews after the games.

Occasionally he breaks loose with the emotion of a fan when he objects to an umpire's decision. "He's really something," says fellow announcer Phil Schaefer. "There'll be a close play at second with the runner called out and Joe will scream, 'He was safe by ten feet.' "

Walker attends the games equipped with a radio so he can listen to the announcers' play-by-play, and he takes notes on all that is happening. He does his interviews on tape for replay and his wife reads the results to him for the daily broadcasts.

The 51-year-old Walker, father of four, grew up in Miami and has been involved with sports from the time he was 10 and played baseball. "I was a left-handed shortstop and second baseman," Walker said.

So what makes Joe Walker so special? Well, there is a big difference between him and the rest of the media. Joe Walker is blind! He has been since birth. "We played baseball with a ball that had a bell on it," he said matter-of-factly. "The bases had bells, too. We ran to a sound."

And when Joe Walker takes notes, he takes them in braille.